Entrepreneurship and Economic Change

Entrepreneurship and Economic Change

Martin Binks
Department of Economics
University of Nottingham

Philip Vale
Department of Management Studies
University of Glasgow

McGRAW-HILL BOOK COMPANY

London · New York · St Louis · San Francisco · Auckland
Bogotá · Guatemala · Hamburg · Lisbon · Madrid · Mexico
Montreal · New Delhi · Panama · Paris · San Juan · São Paulo
Singapore · Sydney · Tokyo · Toronto

Published by
McGRAW-HILL Book Company (UK) Limited
Shoppenhangers Road
Maidenhead · Berkshire · England
Telephone Maidenhead (0628) 23432
Cables MCGRAWHILL MAIDENHEAD Telex 848484
Fax 0628 35895

British Library Cataloguing in Publication Data
Binks, Martin
    Entrepreneurship and economic change.
    1. Economics. Concepts: Entrepreneurship
    I. Title II. Vale, Philip A
    338'.04

    ISBN 0-07-707218-9

Library of Congress Cataloging-in-Publication Data
    Binks, Martin.
    Entrepreneurship and economic change / Martin Binks, Philip Vale.
        p.   cm.
    Includes bibliographical references.
    ISBN 0-07-707218-9
    1. Entrepreneurship. 2. Small business. 3. New business
enterprises. 4. Economics. I. Vale, Philip A.
    II. Title.
HB615.B56   1990
338'.04—dc20   89-35314

12345   B & S   93210

Typeset by Computape (Pickering) Limited, North Yorkshire
and printed and bound in Great Britain by Billings & Sons Limited

For Jessica, Laura, and Alice

CONTENTS

Acknowledgements ix
Introduction 1

PART I THE IDENTIFICATION OF ENTREPRENEURSHIP 5
Introduction 7
Chapter 1 Entrepreneurship: some attempts at identification 9
Chapter 2 The contribution of Joseph Schumpeter 22
Chapter 3 Leibenstein's Theory of Entrepreneurship 31
Chapter 4 Towards a synthesis 40

PART II FACTOR MARKET ANALYSIS 51
Introduction 53
Chapter 5 The factor market for entrepreneurship 57
Chapter 6 The factor market for finance 74
Chapter 7 The factor markets for secondary inputs 88
Chapter 8 Entrepreneurship and economic cycles—a synthesis 105

PART III POLICY AND INFORMATION 123
Introduction 125
Chapter 9 Policy for entrepreneurship 127
Chapter 10 Policy and finance 139
Chapter 11 Policy for secondary inputs 152
Chapter 12 The collection of information 159
In conclusion 171
A resumé of the major tenets of this theory of entrepreneurship 175

Index 177

ACKNOWLEDGEMENTS

The authors gratefully acknowledge the support provided by Rosemary Kwiecinski for her help in compiling the manuscript, Kevin Keasey for his invaluable advice and Julie Ganner for her patience and encouragement.

INTRODUCTION

The main objective of this book is to clarify the contribution of entrepreneurship to economic activity. We have chosen to do so by reference to observations and arguments which provide consistent linkages between definition, theoretical elements, practical necessities, and policy options.

There is neither an uncontested understanding of the role that entrepreneurship plays within the economy nor a universally accepted meaning of the term. Implicit in the rhetoric of speakers encouraging entrepreneurship, and small and new businesses in particular, is the suggestion that their proliferation would increase the aggregate amount of enterprise within the economy and that enterprise is, in some unspecified sense, good for the economy. It would be inferred from this that enterprise promotes economic development, growth, employment generation, and social welfare simultaneously. From the standpoint of a politician viewing an economy that is performing badly and where rates of economic growth and employment levels are low, it is therefore reasonable to advocate enterprise and entrepreneurship if they can be promoted with policy initiatives and the rewards from these exceed the economic cost. The focus of this work is on the economic contribution and role of entrepreneurship in order to identify constraints on entrepreneurial activity and to suggest policies that are focused and efficient.

There are various definitions of entrepreneurship, with associated theoretical observations, the history of which predates much formal economic theory. The natural focus upon individual ideas and enterprise has also encouraged the study of new and small firms as being representative of entrepreneurial activity. In their attempts to promote entrepreneurship, policy designers have presented a variety of initiatives in many countries, most of which concentrate on the encouragement of individuals and new or small firms. The definitional and theoretical debate is largely ignored by those who are concerned with the practical aspects of starting and running small firms. Similarly, the process of policy design has failed to reflect a coherent strategy or evolution because the terms of reference are not clearly identified or understood, and thus there has been little consistent informational support.

The accumulation of empirical evidence which refers to entrepreneurship has been generated in an *ad hoc* manner as a consequence of the general absence of a systematic approach to the subject. Much of the growing body of evidence is relevant and informative, but is only revealing in a disconnected way, with great depth of explanation in some aspects and superficial or non-existent coverage in others.

The present absence of a coherent framework for analytical consideration is largely explained by the dynamic nature of the entrepreneurial process. The character of entrepreneurship is determined by prevailing economic conditions and its realization necessarily changes those conditions. It is therefore, in a sense, futile to attempt to construct a 'model' of entrepreneurial behaviour, since this could never apply to specific economic conditions without losing its relevance to others. It is, however, useful to construct a framework which encompasses the present disparate channels of enquiry in a dynamic way in order to clarify the position and contribution of each in the context of the others.

The book is presented in three parts which broadly reflect the movement from theory through practice to policy.

In Part One we use certain definitional and theoretical constructs from the works of others. The selection is deliberately restricted and serves to distil the salient sources of debate which permeate the literature on entrepreneurship. In presenting this information we raise the key questions surrounding the relationship between entrepreneurship and economic change: whether entrepreneurship causes economic development, merely facilitates it, or simply refers to any form of business management. These elements are presented as complementary facets of the process rather than mutually exclusive alternatives. Part One concludes with a synthesis which indicates the need for analytical clarity to isolate different classes of entrepreneurial event rather than focusing upon the individuals who instigate them.

In Part Two the entrepreneurial categories identified are considered in terms of the main factor markets which they confront and the constraints which would be expected to obtain. The underlying thesis here is that the prediction of certain classes of entrepreneurship is rendered impossible by definition. It is sensible to consider the economic conditions which they face on emergence, however, since if these are found to represent significant constraints to novel enterprise, and if it is assumed that such enterprise is desirable, then the analysis will provide indications of the necessary policy focus required to alleviate the problems arising.

Part Two concludes with a consideration of the preceding observations in terms of their implications for economic activity at a macroeconomic level.

This requirement arises from the modifications to the theory of economic development provided by Joseph Schumpeter, and the theory of economic cycles contained therein.[1] Having changed some of Schumpeter's basic assumptions on the nature of economic relationships pertaining to the impact of entrepreneurial activity upon economic development, it is necessary to reinterpret his analysis of cycles to explain why entrepreneurship is still relevant to their explanation.

Part Three provides a discussion of the policy implications arising from the constraints identified in the factor market analysis in Part Two. The observations which are naturally required for such considerations represent a brief synopsis of relevant issues rather than an attempt at comprehensive coverage. It is important that these observations be made, however, since they complete our aim of an internally consistent approach from abstract theory to policy.

Our final contribution in Part Three refers to the crucial role of information, both in the context of entrepreneurial decisions and more importantly, here, in the case of policy design, since it is the recent upsurge in intervention in this most sensitive area of economic activity that provoked this text.

Our approach prohibits the inclusion of empirical data for two main reasons. First, the volume of empirical observation needed to substantiate each element of the many arguments involved would be colossal, and thus, would impede the clarity of the overall thesis. Second, and more significantly, much of the evidence and information required is unavailable, and thus the coverage would be incomplete, and often too temporally specific.

The emphasis here is upon clarity of argument rather than a detailed examination of each constituent part. This is not a reference book about definitions and theories of entrepreneurship, new and small firms' research findings, or policy initiatives, but an attempt to bring together certain aspects of each to complete an analysis which is theoretically identified, practically considered and operationally relevant in terms of policy design. What emerges is an attempt to synthesize and distil the relevant elements of the authors' experience of the interrelated but hitherto unconnected areas of entrepreneurship. Our approach is therefore ambitious, deliberately provocative and necessarily incomplete in exploring the full implications of the arguments presented. We offer the observations which follow in the hope of promoting debate and creating a more coherent framework within which the positive contribution of entrepreneurship can be encouraged.

REFERENCES

1. Schumpeter, J. A., *The Theory of Economic Development*, Harvard University Press, Cambridge, Mass., 1934.

THE IDENTIFICATION OF ENTREPRENEURSHIP

INTRODUCTION TO PART ONE

The objective of this section of the text is to highlight the main elements of debate about the nature and economic role of entrepreneurship and provide an internally consistent reconciliation of opposing views. This is achieved by focusing upon some of the key figures in the historical debate, in Chapter 1, and then providing a more detailed analysis of the contributions by Joseph Schumpeter in Chapter 2 and Harvey Leibenstein in Chapter 3.

These examples are sufficient to identify the salient components of disagreement in interpretation and provide the foundation for a synthesis in Chapter 4. Here, we explain that it is sensible to depict entrepreneurial events according to three different categories of economic contribution. Having isolated and identified the central elements of entrepreneurship, it is then possible to proceed to Part Two and consider how they relate to the factor markets which they confront.

ENTREPRENEURSHIP: SOME ATTEMPTS AT IDENTIFICATION

The purpose of this chapter is to highlight some of the more conceptual observations about entrepreneurship, which have emerged from the works of other economists. This is necessary in order to identify the issues raised which are most relevant to the analysis which follows in subsequent chapters.

The approach is highly selective since our objective is clarity in terms of our own arguments, rather than a comprehensive coverage of an area which has been presented already by other authors such as Hebert and Link.[1]

In our coverage of past contributions on the subject of entrepreneurship, it is tempting to follow one of two courses. The first would be to take a simple historical perspective which isolates the main conceptual additions made by the large variety of contributors. Since many authors have incorporated similar observations in their discussions, this approach risks both repetition and a lack of clarity in terms of the issues involved. The alternative is to focus upon the main areas of debate which, while isolating the various elements involved, detract from their historical context.

We have chosen to focus upon specific historical considerations whilst also expounding on particular concepts in order to explore them more carefully.

RICHARD CANTILLON (1680?–1734)

The first use of the term entrepreneur in an economic context is attributed to Richard Cantillon in his 'Essai sur la nature de commerce en général'.[2] The time of writing is uncertain but it was first published in 1755, twenty-one years after he died.

Cantillon cites the entrepreneur as any individual who operates under conditions where expenditures are known and certain, but incomes are unknown and uncertain. The uncertainty of income arises because future market demand is not perfectly predictable. It should be clear that 'income', in this context, refers to sales revenues.

Leaving aside, for the moment, the theoretical role of the entrepreneur, it is clear that Cantillon's implicit definition is very broad. The uncertainty to which he refers does not arise because the product or process is necessarily untried and untested. It refers to all economic actions where the commitment to expenditure is made prior to knowing the amount which will result from sales. The unique characteristic of Cantillon's entrepreneur is foresight and the confidence to operate under conditions of uncertainty. Since they were agents who, in his examples, often only confronted single markets, many traders who make daily transactions could constitute entrepreneurs by his definition. This is somewhat unhelpful as it enables the incorporation of a very large proportion of economic decision-makers.

To understand more clearly the entrepreneur which Cantillon proposes, it is helpful to consider one possible interpretation of his motives in more detail. In speculating on Cantillon's motive two aspects can be noted. Turning first to Cantillon's background and character, it is very clear that Cantillon was a natural trader and dealer with a relatively shrewd approach to opportunistic profit. His success as a speculator reveals his ability to perceive and predict the actions and reactions of other speculators better than they could predict his own. This reveals a character which combines an intelligence and perceptiveness with a willingness to take risks. The fact that his perception is uncluttered by social mores and class rigidities is reflected in his admission of individuals from any class, background or activity to the status of entrepreneur, if their actions fall within his definition of entre-preneurship. It is quite plausible that Cantillon, as an individual, regarded the risk which he associated with entrepreneurial decision-making as an attractive aspect of the activity.

From the context in which Cantillon was writing, it is clear that most individuals were easily categorized into two separate groups, employers or employees. His objective might have been to draw the simple distinction between those whose incomes were contracted, and those who provided the contracts, combining the labour with other factors of production. There may, however, have been a more specific motive for the definition put forward by Cantillon. There was a third group of individuals whose contribution to production was not overt or explicit. Since Cantillon was himself a speculator and thus far removed from the operation of the production process, or even the allocation of factors of production to it, it is conceivable that part of his objective was to give a name and therefore a role, and even respectability, to those whose contribution is unobservable and intangible. Cantillon successfully associates risk and uncertainty with the administrative decision-making processes of entrepreneurs. He also identifies the entrepreneurial income or profit which arises through decision-making and risk-taking rather than 'orthodox effort'.

JEAN-BAPTISTE SAY (1767–1832)

Aside from being the first Professor of Economics in Europe, Jean-Baptiste Say also ran his own business. The definition which he provided places the entrepreneur in a much more specialized and detailed role than had been achieved by Cantillon and others who had used the term prior to Say's contribution.[3] Since he would have been an entrepreneur by his own definition, it is perhaps unsurprising that he described a somewhat flattering set of characteristics to isolate the entrepreneur. On the qualities required for successful entrepreneurship, Say wrote that the entrepreneur must have:

> judgement, perseverance and a knowledge of the world as well as of business. He is called upon to estimate, with tolerable accuracy, the importance of the specific product, the probable amount of the demand, and the means of its production at one time, he must employ a great number of hands; at another, buy or order the raw material, collect labourers, find consumers, and give at all times a rigid attention to order and economy; in a word, he must possess the art of superintendence and administration.[4]

Say regards the entrepreneur as a rare phenonemon who is able to co-ordinate and combine the factors of production. The overriding characteristic of the condition in which the entrepreneur operates is the variety of inputs and markets which confront the entrepreneur and which by definition must be successfully combined. The emphasis is not restricted to the final product's market, or the case of transactions that involve buying and selling-on for anticipated profit. The entrepreneur is confronted by the other factor markets such as those for raw materials, labour, finance, land, and plant and equipment. The judgement required to perceive and realize potential arbitrage is only the first of many requirements. The fact that the calculation now refers to a number of different markets implies that the calculation of potential profit from arbitrage is far more complex than under the simpler system portrayed by Cantillon.

Say also appreciated the role of uncertainty and by implication, risk. The following quote illustrates:

> In the course of such complex operations there are an abundance of obstacles to be surmounted, of anxieties to be repressed, of misfortunes to be repaired, and of expedients to be devised.[5]

The entrepreneur is portrayed as being almost a specialist at accommodating the unexpected and overcoming problems.

Say's main motive for defining the entrepreneur in such an explicit and descriptive way may have been to ensure that the full richness and scope of entrepreneurial requirements was made clear. Say appeared concerned that the large number of very different characteristics required in order to be an entrepreneur should not be missed. His emphasis on the many qualities required for entrepreneurship has a final caveat: qualities had to be exhibited simultaneously if the entrepreneurship was to be successful. If any of the isolated qualities were to be missing, then the implication presented is that the entrepreneurial exercise would fail.

From these early contributions, it is very clear that the activities of entrepreneurs were intrinsically bound up with those of the market process. Without their actions the market process could never change but since the conditions of demand and supply are dynamic it would therefore eventually crumble. A natural extension from this position was to consider the role of the entrepreneur in the adjustment process. Entrepreneurs were the conveyors of the market process in a condition of perpetual disequilibrium. It is this conceptual identity which underlies much of the work subsequently undertaken by the Austrian and neo-Austrian schools of economic thought.

SOME AUSTRIAN AND NEO-AUSTRIAN OBSERVATIONS

The crucial role of the entrepreneur in directing and redirecting resources in a state of perpetual disequilibrium was emphasized by the founding father of the Austrian school, Carl Menger (1840–1921).[6] He placed the production process within a hierarchical structure where finished products constituted low-level goods, and primary inputs which were further removed from final production, were higher-order goods. Within this context the entrepreneur was portrayed as being one of the highest orders since they determined the allocation of inputs of lower orders and the pattern of outputs which resulted. He emphasized the entrepreneur's need for information and an ability to analyse that successfully in order to allocate resources correctly. He also therefore highlighted the role of uncertainty in the entrepreneurial process. By implication the entrepreneur is also a risk-bearer and it was this characteristic, along with those of leadership and alertness, which was emphasized by one of Menger's followers, Friedrich Von Wieser (1851–1926).[7]

These qualities were later taken up by Israel Kirzner,[8] who emphasizes that it is the alertness and superior perception of entrepreneurs which cause factors of production to be reallocated towards an equilibrium condition. Kirzner would deny that the equilibrium is ever obtained in practice, and emphasizes the need to concentrate attention upon the adjustment path along which the entrepreneur operates, rather than the equilibrium condition which they are pursuing. Kirzner also argues that the ownership of capital is not necessary to provoke its movement or change of application. In this sense he departs from the orthodoxy of the Austrian tradition.

The small selection of observations presented above are sufficient to convey the essence of the Austrian/neo-Austrian perspective. Their motives in defining and discussing the nature of the entrepreneur reflect the need to provide an identity to the decision-maker who is responsible for pursuing the ever-elusive equilibrium between demand and supply: elusive because demand and supply conditions are always changing.

This necessary role of the entrepreneur as an intrinsic feature of the adjustment process was circumvented in traditional neo-classical analysis by focusing on comparative statics or contrasting equilibria.

THE NEO-CLASSICAL EXCLUSION

The predominance of the neo-classical approach to economic analysis and comparative statics leaves little room for the entrepreneurial function, since it focuses attention on equilibria and the circular flow, and away from the adjustment process.

Although the neo-classical school do not explicitly deny the existence of the entrepreneur, it is almost irrelevant to consider entrepreneurs in the context of neo-classical analysis, since their operations refer to the adjustment processes which are assumed to be instantaneous for the purposes of analytical clarity. The acceptance of neo-classical analysis does much to explain the neglect of entrepreneurship from most popular economic analysis.[9]

Despite the neo-classical evasion, the notion of adjustment and its speed are clearly crucial in attempting to explain the economic contribution of entrepreneurs. Since the adjustment process refers to the allocation and reallocation of factor inputs, it would seem sensible to argue that those responsible for the adjustment, in this case the entrepreneurs, must also be capitalists, since they clearly have the ability to control the allocation of plant and equipment.

These observations raise a central point of debate in the context of entrepreneurship; that is, whether the entrepreneur should be assumed to be a capitalist. Since this question has already arisen and will continue to feature in the analysis which follows, it is necessary to question briefly the nature of capital.

THE AWKWARD QUESTION OF CAPITAL

Many approaches to the definition of capital restrict their notion to that of heritable wealth: a facility that allows the control of tangible productive potential through transferable ownership.

Alternative approaches recognize the potential to invest in human capital. Significant difficulties can emerge from the latter interpretation of capital: immediately it is more difficult to distinguish income accruing to the entrepreneurs' holding of human capital. The usefulness of an opportunity-cost approach is restricted if the next best employment for an entrepreneur is in another unknown entrepreneurial activity.

In the process of perpetual adjustment depicted by the Austrian schools, investment in human capital alters human perception and therefore enables them to adjust more accurately to disequilibrium. It may provide them with the alertness and superior perception to which Kirzner refers. At a more pragmatic level, human capital can enhance credibility among the controllers of non-human capital and facilitate the temporary use of conventional plant and equipment, for application to an entrepreneurial endeavour. The implications of this approach, however, would be the subsequent difficulty of attributing the risk of failure between the owner of human capital and the owner of conventional capital. This approach would also suggest, however, that given sufficient investment in human capital, an individual need not necessarily be a capitalist in the conventional sense of owning tangible capital, i.e. plant and equipment or other assets, in order to pursue an entrepreneurial event or to cause the reallocation of such capital.

From the above discussion it is therefore possible to reconcile the two apparently opposing views, one which considers that the entrepreneur must be a capitalist by definition and the other which suggests that they may be able to influence the allocation of capital without owning it themselves. These views are only in conflict in as much as they fail to differentiate between human capital investment and investment in other forms of capital. Clearly, given sufficient aptitude and investment in human capital, it is quite conceivable that an individual receives income from providing ideas to others, who subsequently incorporate them in entrepreneurial activities. They thus influence the allocation and reallocation of conventionally defined capital assets.

THE CRUCIAL CONTRIBUTION OF JOSEPH SCHUMPETER

It is already becoming clear that some of the confusions and disagreements between contributors on the nature of entrepreneurship arise from a lack of clarity in their definition of concepts. Some of these problems of interpretation and judgement are eliminated if we consider a more restricted but instructive view of entrepreneurship, which raises a new set of questions and hypotheses. This was provided in the work of Joseph Schumpeter.[10] Although we will return to consider his theoretical contributions and their implications in more detail in Chapter 2, it is helpful to introduce some of his contentious interpretations at this point, along with certain more modern interpretations.

Schumpeter's entrepreneur was clearly no one category of person, but a conceptual abstraction which introduced the notion of 'new combinations'. The entrepreneur provided a new product or new production process via a different and hitherto untried combination of inputs. The entrepreneurial element only existed for as long as the introduction of the new combination of inputs was under way. The following quote from his book *The Theory of Economic Development* explains:

> Whatever the type, everyone is an entrepreneur only when he actually carries out new combinations and loses that character as soon as he has built up his business, when he settles down to running it as other people run their business.[11]

He avoids the issue of the exclusive entrepreneurial character by proceeding to observe that:

> This is the rule, of course, and hence it is just as rare for anyone to remain an entrepreneur throughout the decades of his active life as it is for a business man never to have a moment in which he is an entrepreneur, to however modest a degree.[12]

Entrepreneurial events involve a change in product or process which is discrete rather than constituting a gradualistic evolvement of design. The emphasis of Schumpeter's definition therefore rests upon discontinuity rather than gradual or smooth change. He is concerned with irreversible leaps in perception which constitute new combinations and organizations of factors of production as opposed to the gradual development of existing methods.

The real essence of Schumpeter's entrepreneur emerges very clearly if his concept is placed within the framework provided by 'Catastrophe Theory'.

SCHUMPETER'S ENTREPRENEUR AS A PRECURSOR OF 'CATASTROPHE THEORY'

The close similarity between Schumpeter's concept of entrepreneurship and the essential characteristics of 'Catastrophe Theory' is revealed quite clearly in the following quotes, the first from Schumpeter's *The Theory of Economic Development*, and the second from Woodcock and Davis's particularly clear exposition in *Catastrophe Theory*:

> The author begs to add another more exact definition, he is in the habit of using: what we are about to consider is that kind of change arising from within the system which so displaces its equilibrium point that the new one cannot be reached from the old one by infinitesimal steps.[13]

> Catastrophe Theory is a controversial new way of thinking about change . . . it proposes that the mathematics underlying three hundred years of science, though powerful and successful, have encouraged a one-sided view of change. These mathematical principles are ideally suited to analyse—because they were created to analyse—smooth, continuous, quantitative change: . . . but there is another kind of change, too, change that is less suited to mathematical analysis: the abrupt bursting of a bubble, the discontinuous transition from ice at its melting point to water at its freezing point, the qualitative shift in our minds when we 'get' a pun or a play on words . . . discontinuity and qualitative change occur everywhere in thought, language and perception.[14]

In his conceptualization of entrepreneurship as a discrete, causally irreversible discontinuity in the nature of production resulting from a new idea, perception, and realization, Schumpeter provided an exact example of Catastrophe Theory, thirty years before the term was invented.

Schumpeter is quite blatant in defining the entrepreneur in such a way as to be entirely consistent with the key role he envisages the entrepreneur playing in the process of economic development. This introduced an entirely new conceptual framework wherein the entrepreneur causes rather than facilitates economic development. The true entrepreneur is no longer portrayed as the purveyor of market forces or the adjustment process given a new set of demand or supply conditions. The entrepreneur causes the change in the pattern of factor allocation rather than responding to a requirement for that reallocation.

In recognition of this fundamental disagreement as to the economic contribution of the entrepreneur and their role in economic development, Harvey Leibenstein attempted a reconciliation by producing a combination of definitions, rather than one single and restricted version.

LEIBENSTEIN'S SYNTHESIS

Leibenstein's contribution to the theory of entrepreneurship is considered in depth in Chapter 3. It is necessary to introduce the elements of his definition at this point however, in order to help complete this introductory background picture. Leibenstein's first formal theoretical observations on entrepreneurship were published in 1968, although many of the concepts on which these observations rested were published in the 1960s.[15] Leibenstein like Say, emphasizes the need for the successful entrepreneur to synchronize inputs from several different markets.

> If six inputs are needed to bring to fruition a firm that produces a marketable product, it does no good to be able to market five of them. The gap-filling and the input-completing capacities are the unique characteristics of the entrepreneur.[16]

The aspect of the debate which Leibenstein's analysis usefully introduces is the distinction between two types of entrepreneur. On the one hand there is Schumpeter's entrepreneur who arranges new combinations, while on the other hand there is a managerial function for entrepreneurs who establish or run businesses and can, more or less successfully, organize traditional combinations. This distinction between possible roles is fundamental to the discussion of entrepreneurship presented in Chapter 4.

To bring the picture up to date, for historical purposes, it is interesting to consider the definitions provided by Mark Casson and Peter Drucker.

MARK CASSON

In response to the contemporary popularity of entrepreneurship and the associated problems of definition, Mark Casson provided one of the more recent contributions in 1982.[17] He distinguishes two approaches to definition. The first is the functional approach and the second is the indicative approach. The difference between the two is best revealed in the following quotes:

> In the context of the entrepreneur the functional approach says quite simply that an entrepreneur is what an entrepreneur does. It specifies a certain function and deems

anyone who performs this function to be an entrepreneur. The indicative approach provides a description of the entrepreneur by which he may be recognised. Unlike a functional definition, which may be quite abstract, an indicative definition is very down to earth. It describes an entrepreneur in terms of his legal status, his contractual relation with other parties, his position in society and so on.[18]

Casson claims that part of the difficulty in defining entrepreneurship arises from a failure to integrate these two approaches. His argument attempts to integrate them and he presents the following definition as a formal version for application in the rest of his analysis: 'An entrepreneur is someone who specialises in taking judgemental decisions about the coordination of scarce resources.'[19]

In a sense this brief coverage of some definitions and their origins has gone full circle in that the more recent example offered by Casson appears to reflect the same or greater generality than that suggested by Richard Cantillon. Casson, however, goes on to defend his definition and explain it in much more detail. The general thrust of his argument is that entrepreneurs are individuals whose specialism and economic contribution refer to the allocation and reallocation of factors of production.

Casson's analysis is both rigorous and useful in its contribution to traditional economic theory. His application of accepted welfare analysis to the various elements of the decision-making process highlights the relationship between risk and the communication of information by synthesizing that relationship in a welfare format. This particular approach is aimed primarily at those economists who apply the analytical approaches used by Casson. It enables certain predictions to be made about entrepreneurial behaviour and the possible strategies which are used by the individual under conditions of uncertainty and incomplete information.

P. F. DRUCKER

A very accessible alternative treatment of entrepreneurship and the entrepreneur has been provided by Drucker in his book *Innovation and Entrepreneurship*.[20] Drucker takes a pragmatic approach with a strong management orientation. Within an intra-corporate context the focus is upon dynamics, rather than comparative statics, and the development of an entrepreneurial ethos that can capitalize on the exploitation of new opportunities. Drucker's definition echoes Kirzner's with the emphasis upon change.

> Entrepreneurs see change as the norm and as healthy. Usually they do not bring about change themselves. But—and this defines the entrepreneur and entrepreneurship—the entrepreneur always searches for change, responds to it, and exploits it as an opportunity.[21]

Implicit through Drucker's contribution is the idea that entrepreneurship is not restricted to one group of individuals. Entrepreneurs are not born with a specific set of characteristics: entrepreneurial behaviour can be developed among the individuals of existing business organizations to provide a competitive advantage. An emphasis is placed on the attitudinal approach required to be effectively entreprencurial and the prospect of reorientating orthodox managerial outlooks towards one that is proactive and opportunity-exploiting.

The definitions adopted by Casson and Drucker contrast sharply and this fact in itself usefully highlights the apparent discrepancies that actually reflect nothing more than the range of context from which entrepreneurship can be investigated. As with Casson's treatment, there are insights to be taken from Drucker which are complementary to the ideas developed in the argument which follows and which reinforce the schema presented. No attempt is made, however, to integrate these contributions within the context of political economies which is investigated here.

SOME CONCLUDING OBSERVATIONS

From the selection of historical contributions presented, two further inferences emerge. First, there are at least three types of entrepreneur. Second, it is more helpful to focus upon entrepreneurial events rather than the individuals who carry them out.

The three categories of entrepreneur which appear to have been identified in the historical development of the concept are as follows:

1. Entrepreneurs have been identified as reactive. They respond to market signals and in doing so convey and facilitate the market process. They are the agents of adjustment.
2. A second interpretation of the economic contribution of entrepreneurs is almost the exact reversal of this first category and refers to those who cause economic development by introducing and innovating ideas which fundamentally rearrange the allocation of factors of production.
3. The third category of entrepreneurs may be introduced as a result of Leibenstein's work. This would refer to those who, in their management, cause improvements of a gradual nature to existing products and processes. They do more than merely purvey the market process, they change it but in a gradualistic rather than a fundamental manner.

These categories are explored in more detail at the end of Part One in Chapter 4.

Most, but not all of the above contributions refer to entrepreneurs, and therefore, by implication, to individuals. This automatically implies that any group of individuals may be categorized as entrepreneurs or non-entrepreneurs. It might be expected that a considerable degree of movement between the two groups occurs in practice. As Schumpeter suggested many individuals may, by his definition, be entrepreneurial for a short period of time. Since our concern is with the economic impact of entrepreneurship we prefer to focus attention where possible upon entrepreneurial events rather than individuals. This is an important departure from most of the literature surrounding entrepreneurship which focuses attention upon the character- istics and behaviour of the entrepreneurs themselves. It is vital, for a clear perception of many of the arguments which follow, that emphasis is placed upon the events which constitute entrepreneurship and not their individual perpetrators. It is an unnecessary and restrictive distraction, for our analysis, to explain the sociological and psychological considerations of the impact of changing economic conditions upon the propensity of individuals to be entre- preneurial. This is also a monumental task for which we, as economists, are not qualified. The term 'entrepreneur' is not superfluous, however, it simply refers to the instigator of entrepreneurial events for so long as they occur.

It is now necessary to summarize the extent to which previous definitions of entrepreneurship and the entrepreneur are useful in the present context.

The recent upsurge in attention given to the role of the entrepreneur indicated in our introduction arises primarily from the perceived need to achieve certain objectives by encouraging entrepreneurial activity. These objectives, though unclearly stated from a policy standpoint, refer primarily to employment creation and economic development through industrial restructuring. At present there is a perceived need for more entrepreneurs and more entrepreneurial events but it is unclear how the contribution by entrepreneurs is to be made and how an increasing number of entrepreneurs is to be facilitated. None of the definitions presented above refers explicitly to employment creation. Some refer quite clearly to the process of economic development, but there is a failure to make a clear distinction between the process of economic development and any associated employment. Similarly, there is a failure to recognize that entrepreneurs, as defined by some theorists, do not generate economic development. The simplification that entre- preneurs, economic development, and employment creation are all part of an 'enterprise package' has led to the formulation of policies which fail to accommodate the mechanisms of development and employment. Many policies purporting to encourage entrepreneurship can be viewed simply as attempts to create additional employment. This may be counter-productive in terms of economic development as our arguments imply.

A primary objective of the analysis which follows is to consider the extent to which entrepreneurship enables economic development. It is necessary that the definition of entrepreneurship accommodate the range of economic events which could loosely be described as entrepreneurial. From the preceding discussion it emerges that there is not so much disagreement over the term entrepreneur, as a failure to suggest that an individual may be more or less likely to promote an entrepreneurial event and, unconnected to that propensity, that there could be a variable degree of entrepreneurship embodied within any particular event.

The impact and frequency of entrepreneurial events associated with any particular person will determine how closely that individual approximates to the conceptual construct of the 'entrepreneur'. Whether or not it is worth pursuing the entrepreneur further will be determined by any scheme that can be devised to explain their role within an economy. Relying on a categorization of entrepreneurial events, however, does allow an aggregation of the work discussed and suggests how the definitions and analysis of previous writers can be presented as part of a complementary whole rather than as a collection of conflicting insights.

For the purposes of the analysis which follows, entrepreneurial activity is defined as: 'An unrehearsed combination of economic resources instigated by the uncertain prospect of temporary monopoly profit.'

As is self-evident, this definition quite closely follows the conceptual construct provided by Joseph Schumpeter. The combination of resources is unrehearsed; it has not existed previously. The motive for rehearsing it, or innovating it for the first time, is one of monopoly profit. There is, however, an element of uncertainty in that prospect.

It is now possible to proceed to a closer analysis of two of the major contributions most useful in clarifying our arguments, one by Joseph Schumpeter and the other by Harvey Leibenstein. The chapter which follows on the theory provided by Joseph Schumpeter is a logical, as well as consistent, continuation from the definitional stance we have adopted above.

REFERENCES

1. Hebert, R. and Link, A., *The Entrepreneur*, Praeger, New York, 1982.
2. Cantillon, R. (1755), 'Essai sur la nature du commerce en général', ed. H. Higgs, Macmillan, London, 1931.
3. Say, J. B., quoted in A. H. Cole, 'The entrepreneur: introductory remarks', in H. J. G. Aitken (ed.), *Explorations in Enterprise: an approach to the study of entrepreneurship*, Harvard University Press, Cambridge, Mass., 1965, pp. 32–33.
4. Ibid.
5. Ibid.
6. Menger, C., *Principles of Economics*, trans. J. Dingwall, B. F. Hoselitz, Free Press, Glencoe, 1950.
7. Wieser, F. von, *Social Economics*, trans. A. F. Hindrichs, Adelphi, New York, 1927.
8. Kirzner, I. M., *Competition and Entrepreneurship*, University of Chicago Press, Chicago, 1973.
9. Baumol, W. J., 'Entrepreneurship in economic theory', *American Economic Review* (Papers and Proceedings), **58**, 1968, pp. 64–71.
10. Schumpeter, J. A., *The Theory of Economic Development*, Harvard University Press, Cambridge, Mass. 1934.
11. Ibid., p. 78.
12. Ibid.
13. Ibid., p. 64.
14. Woodcock, A. and Davis, M., *Catastrophe Theory*, Pelican Books, London, 1980.
15. Leibenstein, H. 'Entrepreneurship and development', *American Economic Review*, **58**, 1968, pp. 72–83.

16. Ibid.
17. Casson, M. *The Entrepreneur: An Economic Theory*, Martin Robertson, Oxford, 1982.
18. Ibid., p. 23.
19. Ibid.
20. Drucker, P. F., *Innovation and Entrepreneurship*, Pan Books, London, 1986.
21. Ibid., p. 42.

TWO

THE CONTRIBUTION OF JOSEPH SCHUMPETER

The definition of entrepreneurship provided at the end of Chapter 1 is consistent with the depiction adopted by Joseph Schumpeter. As will emerge more clearly in Chapter 4, our focus upon events rather than individuals enables a categorization approach according to relative entrepreneurial content. By rendering the actions of different economic agents distinct in terms of the entrepreneurial content involved, it is possible to consider the ways in which each category might be constrained since this may vary between categories. This provides a more reliable foundation on which to design policy because it makes more explicit the type of event which is to be influenced, and the likely entrepreneurial impact as indicated by the category concerned.

Since the common link between each category of event will refer to the greater or lesser complement of Schumpeterian entrepreneurship which it embodies, it is sensible to review some of the key elements of his theory. Given that Schumpeter's concern was directed primarily at explaining economic development rather than entrepreneurship, it is necessary to extend and modify some aspects of the analysis for the purpose here. The extent to which what follows is consistent or inconsistent with Schumpeter's analysis is reviewed at the end of this chapter. Consider, however, some of the main characteristics of Schumpeter's theory as they emerge from his major contributions in the 1930s.[1]

THE CIRCULAR FLOW OF ECONOMIC INTERRELIANCE AND ITS CHANGE

The starting point for his theory is the notion of circularity in the flow of economic activity, which is similar to, but not synonymous with, the more conventional macroeconomic notion of the circular flow of income. The underlying principle in his approach is that at any one time all economic activity is interrelated and interdependent. Each seller's market depends on customers finding a market for their contribution in order to generate sufficient purchasing power to provide the vendor's income. According to Schumpeter this economic system will not change capriciously but will, at all times, be connected with the preceding state of affairs. He explains this with reference to Wieser's principle of continuity: it is always possible to associate change in a continuous way from preceding events within the system. This emphasis upon endogeneity does not however, preclude the incidence of events which, in their characteristics, show no clear evolution from existing products or processes. The occurrence of these is central to Schumpeter's theory, though, as we discuss later, he does not explain their cause. Their association is continuous in the sense that they constitute economic development by their essential viability rather than their overt connection to established precedents.

To Schumpeter any enterprise is a combination of many resources. Indeed the whole economic system is simply a large set of established combinations of inputs. Within this system the entrepreneur is one who innovates a new organization or combination of inputs for the first time. As indicated in the first chapter this distinction of the entrepreneur excludes owners and managers of new businesses, for example, who are replicating existing firms.

Schumpeter also emphasizes that the true entrepreneur bears no financial risk. The act of entrepreneurship is distinct from investment and the ownership of capital.

Schumpeter goes on to claim that the circular flow described above changes in two specific ways. The first refers to a gradualistic movement as tastes and populations change and refinements in business are developed. The second refers to spontaneous, discrete or discontinuous, internally generated changes which cannot be progressively associated with their causes. Although they are generated from and within the existing system they bear no observable linkages with preceding combinations. These are not externally generated by exogenous shocks such as acts of God, war or other dramatic influences. An extension of the passage presented in Chapter 1 identifies clearly what Schumpeter regarded as entrepreneurial activity and indeed the requirement for a theory which accommodates it. To quote the footnote in full:

in the first edition of this book, I called it 'dynamics'. But it is preferable to avoid this expression here, since it so easily leads us astray because of the associations which attach themselves to its various meanings. Better, then, to say simply what you mean: economic life changes; it changes partly because of changes in the data, to which it tends to adapt itself. But this is not the only kind of economic change; there is another which is not accounted for by influence on the data without, but which arises from within the system, and this kind of change is the cause of so many important economic phenomena that it seems worthwhile to build a theory for it, and, in order to do so, to isolate it from all the other factors of change. The author begs to add another more exact definition, which he is in the habit of using: what we are about to consider is that kind of change arising from within the system which so displaces its equilibrium point that the new one cannot be reached from the old one by infinitesimal steps. Add successively as many mail coaches as you please, you will never get a railway thereby.[2]

The reason for including some repetition in the quote is to highlight the particular theoretical aspects which he was concerned to emphasize.

Schumpeter goes on to isolate five categories of discrete change that constitute development:

1. the introduction of a new product or quality of product;
2. a new method of production which is unproven;
3. the opening up of a new market to the products already produced in the economy concerned;
4. the opening up or conquest of a new source of raw materials or part manufactured goods;
5. the carrying out of a new organization of industry, for example, creating or destroying a monopoly condition.

Each of these examples of the discrete changes which Schumpeter focuses upon as a source of economic development are important in that they display similar characteristics of sudden change. The implications of this process are considered in more detail after summarizing further some of the associated points which Schumpeter makes.

FINANCING ENTREPRENEURSHIP

Any of these sources of discontinuity require finance. In Schumpeter's model this refers to the power to divert factors of production from their present usage in the circular flow to an essentially new combination. As a result, in Schumpeter's interpretation, interest payments represent the premium on credit which enables this diversion of factor inputs. The entrepreneurial event may be financed by credit alone. In its purest form the model assumes that entrepreneurial activity would require credit since only this would provide that necessary premium. In the absence of accumulated assets the entrepreneur is prepared to pay interest to finance the new combination due to the expectation of *potential* entrepreneurial profit. Schumpeter therefore sees original interest as a tax, or a brake on entrepreneurial profit and thus development. Any positive interest rate implies development foregone where the perceived profit is insufficient or too uncertain to justify the commitment of the potential entrepreneur.

Schumpeter sets out quite clearly to isolate his concept of entrepreneurship from any associated traditionally accepted economic ideas. By divorcing entrepreneurial activity from the ownership or accumulation of wealth, Schumpeter reinforces the earlier point that it does not necessarily involve financial risk to the entrepreneur.

As the initiator of discrete changes and through them, economic development, the entrepreneur is presented by Schumpeter as a key figure in stark contrast to the 'mere manager' of an existing enterprise. Schumpeter emphasizes the distinction between his analysis and that of those who regard the term entrepreneur as an unnecessary distinction. He refers primarily to the work of Alfred Marshall as representative of the traditional economists for whom the entrepreneur is irrelevant. Schumpeter indicates the key role in economic development which entrepreneurs and entrepreneurial activity play and in his terms, therefore, he refutes the stance of traditionalists who consider entrepreneurship as insignificant and merely a part of the natural adjustment process.

RESISTANCE TO ENTREPRENEURSHIP

Schumpeter goes on to identify sources of resistance to entrepreneurial activity and hence economic development. First, the entrepreneur as an individual, i.e. the potential instigator of entrepreneurial activity, may be reluctant to pursue the event for the very reason that the outcome is unknown. This is in line with the concept of opportunity cost providing a natural mechanism for discouraging entrepreneurial activity as an alternative to orthodox employment. Schumpeter also refers to the resistance which naturally exists in society towards accepting the unknown. The entrepreneur's hesitancy may be further compounded because of the anticipated conservative approach taken by institutional and social structures which may be relied upon to provide resources for the venture. He also claimed that inventions which were not commercially innovated were irrelevant. Although consistent with his analysis and objectives, this is an assertion with which we disagree fundamentally for the purpose of our argument, as is explained further below.

PROFIT

One of the most important distinctions which Schumpeter provides in his theory of economic development is the notion of entrepreneurial profit. Since the entrepreneur is a distinct factor of production with respect to development and change, payment to that factor of production will also be distinct.

The important aspect of Schumpeter's notion of entrepreneurial profit lies in its temporariness. By implementing a new 'combination' of factors of production the entrepreneur profits from the advantage of being the first to do so. For example, the innovation of a more efficient production process means that for a time the entrepreneur will be the only producer to reap the benefit of the associated lower unit cost. As information is exchanged, others attempt to emulate the original innovation of the entrepreneur, the entrepreneurial profits are gradually eroded as the mechanism of competition realigns price and costs. Two quotes serve to illustrate the source of entrepreneurial profit and its transience in the context of Schumpeter's own theory.

> They have carried out new combinations. They are entrepreneurs. And their profit, the surplus, to which no liability corresponds, is an entrepreneurial profit.

> And the latter (entrepreneurial profit) and also the entrepreneurial function as such, perish in the vortex of the competition which streams after them.[3]

According to Schumpeter the determination of entrepreneurial profit lies outside traditional marginalist analysis. The entrepreneur cannot predict the profit of an intended new combination: the demand for the output of the enterprise is clearly unpredictable since it is new and therefore there are no previous observations on which to base predictions of the level of demand. Entrepreneurs will also be unaware of the duration of their entrepreneurial profit; they will have no gauge by which to measure the speed at which it will be eroded by the innovations of competitors who follow. The entrepreneur cannot therefore assess the potential of future entrepreneurial activity according to marginalist criteria because the information required is not available. Schumpeter therefore reinforces his rejection of the marginalist tradition in explaining economic development and economic change since it is clearly unable to explain or accommodate the very process by which they are caused.

Schumpeter provides an internally consistent theory of economic development which rests exclusively on the contributions of entrepreneurial activity. The brief summary of this process which follows provides a synthesis of the above points. It also explains why Schumpeter did not proceed further in developing a theory of entrepreneurship since, for the purposes of his analysis, the theory was adequately developed.

DEVELOPMENT AS A CYCLICAL PROCESS

This is an area which is subject to considerable modification in later chapters but it is sufficient, here, to summarize Schumpeter's own view.

Schumpeter did not envisage the development process as a smooth one with entrepreneurial events of common magnitude being distributed evenly through time. He advanced the thesis that cycles in economic activity may be explained by a tendency for entrepreneurial activity to 'cluster'. He envisaged booms in economic activity as being characterized by 'swarms' of entrepreneurs causing structural change.

Although the swarming effect is explained from a variety of viewpoints the most relevant to the analysis here is the relationship between entrepreneurial activity and the natural contextual resistance to entrepreneurship referred to earlier. In a period preceding the cluster of entrepreneurial ventures the absence implies a stable circular flow. The longer that stability obtains the greater the resistance to change. The first entrepreneurial event which is successfully realized has several affects. It disturbs the structure of the circular flow itself and it changes people's perception of change. Entrepreneurial events previously frustrated solely due to the entrenched nature of social, institutional, and political conservatism may now be accepted. This process generates its own momentum. As the stock of viable entrepreneurial events is realized the industrial structure would be expected to adjust.

Ironically in the light of his rejection of the neo-classical approach this process of clustering may be most easily explained by reference to a marginalist approach. Given the appearance of an initial entrepreneurial event, superficially less attractive events may become realizable because of the marginal reduction in the resistance to change brought about by the first event. This process would be expected to continue until the level of resistance to change has dropped to one where the cost of credit became the effective brake on further activity. This would affect the marginal case in a cluster or cohort of entrepreneurial events and signifies the end of a Schumpeterian boom. This does not imply that those entrepreneurial events which are unrealized in one particular boom do not occur at some future point when economic conditions have changed.

An additional extension to the theory provided by Schumpeter refers to the development of Catastrophe Theory as introduced in Chapter 1.

THE CONTRIBUTION OF CATASTROPHE THEORY

The consistency of Schumpeter's theory of economic development and Catastrophe Theory presented earlier can be reinforced with the following quote from V. I. Arnold, which is sufficient to indicate at least a sensible degree of similarity in approach between the two views. On Catastrophe Theory, Arnold states the following:

> If a stable equilibrium state describes the established conditions in some real system (say in economics, ecology or chemistry) then when it cmerges with an unstable equilibrium state, the system must jump to a completely different state: as the parameter is changed the equilibrium condition in the neighbourhood considered suddenly disappears. It was jumps of this kind which lead to the term 'catastrophe theory'.[4]

Catastrophe Theory was developed by Rene Thom in the early 1960s and popularized by his friend E. Christopher Zeeman in the 1970s.[5] The following brief summary of points relevant to this analysis is only sufficient to justify specific related arguments. Those wishing to pursue a fuller understanding of Catastrophe Theory *per se* are recommended to read the contributions by Zeeman,[6] Arnold,[7] and Woodcock and Davis.[8]

The name, Catastrophe Theory, is somewhat misleading as it implies a pejorative element of disaster in the events to which it refers. This is not appropriate. As the quotes have already indicated, Catastrophe Theory refers to discrete rather than continuous phenomena.

As a complement to Newtonian mathematics which focuses upon smooth and continuously changing variables, catastrophe theory considers sudden and irreversible jumps. It explains the occurrence of such fundamental changes in state with reference to the combination, for example, in simplest form, of a normal factor and a splitting factor. By gradually increasing the normal factor with a given level of the splitting factor, a point is reached where the system 'jumps' to a different equilibrium condition. For example, a firm may employ a particular size and genus (technologically) of machine while orders rise. It may meet successive requirements to increase output by using labour more intensively through a shift system or overtime without varying the amount or type of plant and equipment. At some point it will buy another machine of the same type as it already uses, or jump to a different technology with different cost parameters. The purchase of an additional machine would represent a 'catastrophe' or discrete change. The transfer to a different technology would represent a more fundamental catastrophe. Once undertaken, however, the condition cannot be exactly reversed unless *ceteris paribus* the resale price of equipment is the same as the purchase price when new.

In this example, the normal factor is the increase in demand and the splitting factor is the availability of new plant and equipment or a different technology.

Schumpeter's prime concern was with the explanation of economic development and he did not provide a clear indication of the causes of 'insight' that lead to the entrepreneurial events upon which his theory relies so heavily. In this sense his theory of development is incomplete because it fails to explain the central prerequisite of a 'novel idea'. In Schumpeter's perception, such events occurred, and their source or explanation was not so much his concern as their effects. Reference to the framework of Catastrophe Theory at its simplest level is instructive as an extension to Schumpeter's basic model.

Consider for example information as the normal factor and imagination as the splitting factor. To simplify, assume that the stock of imagination is fixed. As the amount of information made available to, or combined with, the stock of imagination is gradually increased, there comes a point when an entirely different perception is enabled which was hitherto inaccessible. This could constitute the source idea for an entrepreneurial event.

This simple model can be expanded to encompass a dynamic element in the nature of information input. With improvements in communication and information technology, the nature of the input may reflect a larger stochastic element. The information set available will reflect, increasingly, the insights of others when in pursuit of unrelated goals. Such insights, however, may enable new perceptions by the recipient which constitute the source ideas for an entrepreneurial event. In this way it is possible to extend Schumpeter's basic model to include a stochastic element with respect to entrepreneurship which still derives from within the overall circular flow but does not constitute a deterministic format for the creation of new ideas since the input of information was not a natural consequence of the endeavours of the individuals concerned.

While its application to a theory of entrepreneurship is necessarily speculative, Catastrophe Theory provides a natural extension to the work of Schumpeter. It enables the formulation and introduction of a stochastic element into the theory of entrepreneurship. This provides a more realistic context for the interpretation and role of policy. By placing entrepreneurial activity in the context of a stochastic structure, the role of policy is highlighted not just in terms of the adjustment process but also in recognition of the creative process. The stochastic principle ensures the separation of entrepreneurial activities of a Schumpeterian form from those which are deterministic or reactive. In this sense it retains Schumpeter's emphasis upon entrepreneurial activity as representing discrete changes in the equilibria existing within the circular flow.

The application of Catastrophe Theory could take place at several points within Schumpeter's general formulation. The first stage refers to the gradual build-up of knowledge and experience which, when it is of sufficient quantity, enables access to what was hitherto unperceivable. This would refer to the process of invention. The second stage refers to the accumulated pressure which builds up in Schumpeter's view behind the inertia to change, engendered in the circular flow. The catastrophic change occurs when the first of the cluster of entrepreneurial events is finally innovated. That catastrophic event then leads to a substantial number of lesser catastrophic changes in different parts of the circular flow as the industrial structure adapts to the various entrepreneurial events which follow the initial breakthrough. These events are clearly related only to the extent that they occur over a short period of time. It is not necessary for them to be sectorily or regionally related.

This adjunct to Schumpeter's theory provides a possible structure for analysing the entrepreneurial process *prior* to the occurrence of its associated event. This introduces the relevance of unrealized entrepreneurial events in that an incomplete prelude in terms of information and imagination could mean that potentially viable development is wasted or lost. Given the concern here, with the need to establish a framework on which to base policy design, this concept of unrealized entrepreneurship is important, since such policies may refer to the engendering of entrepreneurship through the encouragement of information access and imagination. If the policies were successful, entrepreneurial events which might hitherto have been unrecognized will now occur. Assessing the extent to which this occurred in practice would present obvious difficulties. It is impossible to quantify the frequency of 'non-occurrence'.

To clarify this analysis, the extent of acceptance and rejection of Schumpeter's proposals can be summarized as follows.

The approach presented here incorporates, as crucial elements of the argument, the notions of:

1. discrete rather than gradualistic change as the hallmark of entrepreneurship;
2. the role of a 'pioneer' in entrepreneurial activity, but one which is rather different from that envisaged by Schumpeter (Chapter 4);
3. potential temporary monopoly profits as the motive behind entrepreneurship;
4. the possibility that macroeconomic trends will be affected by bursts of entrepreneurial activity, though this again refers to a different process from that envisaged by Schumpeter (Chapter 9).

The main areas of disagreement refer to the following assertions:

1. that unrealized inventions are irrelevant;
2. that entrepreneurship may be devoid of risk;
3. that cycles in economic activity are caused by a 'damburst' of entrepreneurial events as resistance is eroded.

While the reasoning behind some of these observations is obvious from preceding arguments, others will emerge more clearly in future chapters.

Having established the main aspects of Schumpeter's argument which have been adopted for the purposes of this analysis, it is useful to pursue further the issue of different categories of entrepreneurial event. A good starting point is the work of Harvey Leibenstein since he recognized the need for more than one type of entrepreneurial activity, though his analysis is restricted still, by focusing on people rather than events.

REFERENCES

1. Schumpeter, J. A., *The Theory of Economic Development*, Harvard University Press, Cambridge, Mass., 1934; Schumpeter, J. A., *Business Cycles: A Theoretical Historical and Statistical Analysis of the Capitalist Process*, 1st edn. 2nd impression, McGraw-Hill, Maidenhead, 1939.
2. Schumpeter, *Theory*, op. cit., p. 64.
3. Ibid., p. 132.
4. Arnold, V. I., *Catastrophe Theory*, 2nd edn, Springer-Verlag, London, 1986, p. 19.
5. Zeeman, E. C., *Catastrophe Theory Selected Papers*, Addison-Wesley, Reading, Mass., 1972-1977.
6. Ibid.
7. Arnold, *Catastrophe Theory*, op. cit.
8. Woodcock, A. and Davis, M., *Catastrophe Theory*, Pelican Books, London, 1980.

THREE
LEIBENSTEIN'S THEORY OF ENTREPRENEURSHIP

In order to understand the significance of Leibenstein's contribution to the theory of entrepreneurship it is necessary to begin by summarizing his concept of x-efficiency. This was first introduced in his paper in the *American Economic Review* in 1966 entitled 'Allocative efficiency v. "x-efficiency"'.[1] Indeed it is this theoretical construct, rather than his analogous model of entrepreneurship, which is more relevant to our own analysis, hence our greater emphasis upon the nature and credibility of x-efficiency.

X-EFFICIENCY

Leibenstein attempts to draw a distinction between allocative efficiency and other sources of efficiency which he, for convenience, refers to as x-efficiency.

Allocative efficiency refers to the efficiency with which resources and factors of production are combined to satisfy effective demand within an economy. Under conditions of perfect competition in the neo-classical framework, there would be perfect allocative efficiency insofar as no factor could be reallocated to raise the level of welfare for the prevailing distribution of income. Imperfect competition in the neo-classical analysis, such as monopoly, may lead to allocative inefficiency since a higher level of output could be obtained and a higher level of welfare could be attained by a reallocation of resources to competitive firms. Leibenstein argues that allocative inefficiency is not a serious cause of lost welfare and he presents a variety of evidence to substantiate this point. He claims that if monopoly power, i.e. in the form of trade restrictions, were removed, this would not provide substantial benefits. Leibenstein claimed that by eliminating monopoly in the USA, for example, gross national product would rise by about one-thirteenth of 1 per cent.

He also cites evidence which shows many firms to be operating well within their production possibility frontier. This implies that there is a further aspect to efficiency, or a non-allocative efficiency: Leibenstein refers to this as x-efficiency. In this situation x-efficiency does not necessarily reflect a misallocation of resources. His examples refer to industries and firms where the equipment is largely identical in its allocation and operation but where the unit costs differ. Contemporary examples of x-inefficiency might be taken from the output of cars from similar plants in Britain and Europe. A further example from the experience of the UK might refer to the implementation of the 'three-day week' which was applied as a result of the miners' strike in 1974 where the total output dropped by a much smaller proportion than the total time spent in its production. It is Leibenstein's construction of the notion of x-efficiency and its corollary x-inefficiency which is relevant to the analysis which follows. Whereas supporting evidence clearly substantiates the case for different productivity levels, the validity of the concept of x-inefficiency is less clear.

Leibenstein attributes much of the cause of x-inefficiency to differential and inadequate motivation and information usage. Put simply, unless there is pressure to innovate or work harder, firms will allow levels of x-inefficiency to increase. They may be aware of new techniques but not feel it necessary to use them. They may be aware of the potential rewards from improving their knowledge through consultancy, for example, but again not feel that implementation is a necessary requirement for the survival and profitability of their firm.

Leibenstein sets out several categories of motivation, intraplant motivation, external motivation or efficiency, and non-market input efficiency. These refer respectively to the motivation of those individuals within a firm, the motivation of potential and actual competitors in that industry and the use and accumulation of information. Leibenstein states 'the simple fact is that neither individuals nor firms work as hard nor do they search for information as effectively as they could'.

These observations give rise to an important consideration which refers to the relationship between inputs and output. From the evidence submitted in his paper Leibenstein concludes that the production function is not clearly or uniquely specified. For any particular firm or industry the relationship between output and the application of inputs is indeterminate. Leibenstein provides four reasons for this situation. The first refers to the contracts for labour which he claims are not specified precisely in terms of effort to enable the labour input to be uniquely determined. Second, he observes that not all factors of production are actually marketed. Certain aspects of management skill for example may be provided at the discretion of the employee and not automatically when the firm would benefit. Third, the production function for the firm concerned, i.e. the relationship between inputs and output, is not completely specified or known. The firm may be aware of the relationship which exists between the current input patterns and the resulting output levels but does not have access to reliable information on the effects of changes in the input pattern and their potential impact upon output levels. Fourth, competing firms may often co-operate and imitate each other either covertly or overtly rather than compete: there is therefore less incentive for innovation within this 'friendly' form of competition.

Leibenstein's initial identification of the concept of x-efficiency and x-inefficiency underlies many of the theoretical contributions which he subsequently made concerning entrepreneurship. It should be emphasized however that the initial contributions were not prompted by a desire to examine and explain entrepreneurship. In part, his motivation was to provide a critique of the neo-classical view of the market process. There was in the mid-1960s an almost total absence of applied or traditional theoretical contributions which referred primarily to the role of the entrepreneur and entrepreneurship *per se*. In his later work on the theory of entrepreneurship the concept of x-efficiency was to play a central role since it was seen as the prime motive for entrepreneurial actions. In a sense Say's multimarket co-ordination and the prospect of arbitrage by a more effective (more x efficient) combination underlay much of Leibenstein's theory of the instigation of entrepreneurial activity.

Since the concept was developed prior to its application to the area of entrepreneurship, it is necessary to be aware of the criticisms which were levelled at the theory itself before considering how Leibenstein subsequently applied it to entrepreneurial activity.

STIGLER'S CRITIQUE

The main criticisms of Leibenstein's theory of x-efficiency were prompted by its apparent divergence from the neo-classical model. George Stigler provided a fair if somewhat vicious criticism of the underlying principles of Leibenstein's theory.[2] From Stigler's points it emerges that the bulk of Leibenstein's theory is acceptable but for one fundamental flaw: Leibenstein fails to identify the notion of output correctly. To quote Stigler:

> In this case, and in every motivational case, the question is: what is output? Surely no person ever seeks to maximise the output of any one thing: even the single proprietor, unassisted by hired labour, does not seek to maximise the output of corn: he seeks to maximise utility, and surely other products including leisure and health as well as corn enter into his utility function. When more of one goal is achieved at the cost of less of another goal the increase in output due to 'say' increased effort is not an increase in 'efficiency' it is a change in output.[3]

Stigler proceeds to apply a similar format of criticism to many of the aspects which Leibenstein identifies as sources of x-inefficiency.

Stigler's observations would appear to be successful in negating the attack upon conventional neo-classical theory presented by Leibenstein in his theory of x-efficiency. By incorporating a more general notion of utility it is possible to reduce Leibenstein's points to a simple identification of the nature and mismatch between the utility functions of those operating within the firms. These mismatches will necessarily be reflected in different levels of firm's explicit or normal production.

Leibenstein appears to assume that labour inputs to the production function are homogenous. By lifting this assumption the identification of different levels of output from identical factor inputs, with the exception of labour, becomes a point of interest but not significance as far as the validity of the neo-classical tradition is concerned.

X-EFFICIENCY RESTATED

This line of criticism does not necessarily invalidate the importance of the concept of x-efficiency and inefficiency, however, for the purposes of theories of entrepreneurship. In some senses it is still helpful to retain such a concept but restate it as the output implications of the mismatch between the utility functions of the labour inputs in any firm or industry. To simplify, utility functions combine a large number of different and complex trade-offs for any specific individual. In the case of Leibenstein's argument, the main trade-off is between work and leisure. Within this simpler utility framework, effort is seen as influencing the level of production which is related to income and therefore the goods and services which can be used to derive utility. Leisure provides relaxation and that in itself provides utility. Clearly it is unhelpful for practical purposes to attempt to compare the actual utility functions of different individuals; they are unspecified and they change. When individuals are interdependent in the production process their utility functions are almost bound to conflict to some extent. The scale of this effect, in terms of its reflection in production levels, will depend first upon the level of relevant conflict between the utility functions of those involved, and second upon the extent to which the individual operators are interdependent. For example, in the context of an assembly line, the level of production may be directly related to the slowest participant. In terms of the overall level of output, however, there will always be a source of inefficiency since it is safe to assume first, that no two individuals will have the same utility function and second, that nobody will be able fully to perceive the differential utility functions of the economic operators involved in production.

The extent of the production shortfall in this alternative statement of x-inefficiency will reflect the difference between the output levels of a perfectly complementary, homogenous, fully committed workforce and the actual levels which exist. This is clearly impossible to measure. It is, however, a useful consideration in the context of entrepreneurial motivation as applied by Leibenstein. The existence of a shortfall inspires entrepreneurship in a form which attempts first to increase the weight attached to the firm's nominal output, in the utility functions of the workforce and second, to reduce the mismatch between different utility functions and therefore combine the labour factors with other factors of production more effectively.

In the context of Leibenstein's work this restatement of x-efficiency yields an interesting contradiction however. First the competitive pressure which is, from Leibenstein's viewpoint, able to reduce x-inefficiency, operates both inside and outside the firm. Co-operation between interdependent workers within the firm, rather than competition for promotion purposes, could reduce the effective mismatch between utility functions by raising in each individual's utility function the profile and value of 'getting on well' with one's colleagues and thus causing increases in production. It is therefore consistent to assume that increased competition which is provided externally by other firms should in theory increase pressure for co-operation within the firm. This contradicts the notion of competition between individuals within firms in terms of their contribution to output which is motivated by the potential for increased rewards through promotion or other means.

The simple quantification of inputs, assuming homogenous labour, is therefore contradictory to a resultant reliance upon differential motivation as an explanation of x-efficiency. A more useful application of the concept x-efficiency arises from an examination of the sources of differential utility functions which, when combined in a production process, lead to different levels of output.

While the extensions to, and modifications of, Stigler's criticisms of Leibenstein's theory have been provided primarily by the authors, it is clear that Leibenstein did not accept the validity of the criticisms which were directed at his theory. This, in part, is reflected in his future application of the concept to a theory of entrepreneurship. The main characteristics of this theory are summarized in the following paragraphs.

LEIBENSTEIN'S THEORY OF ENTREPRENEURSHIP

Assuming for the present the validity of the x-efficiency paradigm in indicating a cause of 'slack' within the production process, then its very existence implied to Leibenstein the motive for entrepreneurial opportunity. If there were definite and predictable relationships between inputs and outputs and the free movement of factors of production, as indicated and dictated by relative profit levels, then there would clearly be no motive or opportunity for entrepreneurship. The role, according to Leibenstein, of the entrepreneur in development is hidden by the neo-classical competitive model which makes such assumptions.

In his paper 'Entrepreneurship and development'[4] Leibenstein distinguishes between two types of entrepreneur. First, he identifies the entrepreneur as a routine or managerial figure allocating the inputs to the production process in a traditional manner. Second, he refers to the Schumpeterian entrepreneur as one filling an observed market gap by producing a new product or process. The extent to which Leibenstein's Schumpeterian entrepreneur differs from Schumpeter's actual perception of the role of the entrepreneur and the author's extension of that perception, will emerge more clearly in the following chapter.

Leibenstein claims to identify four characteristics in the entrepreneur's role. First, they connect different markets to exploit potential arbitrage. Second, they remove market deficiencies by filling gaps in the market process. Third, they are input completers in that they co-ordinate all of the inputs required for production, and finally, they create or expand firms as productive outlets.

He observes that the skills and abilities required to perform these roles are scarce. He also identifies their realization as to some extent being related to the motivational state of the entrepreneur and their associated workforce. The motivational state is determined by a number of factors. The system of financial reward may appear to provide superior motivation by the application of piece rates, for example. The extent of promotional determinants that are not related to performance, such as the 'old school tie', may have a demotivating effect on those excluded from a particular route; in this case because they went to the wrong school. He also refers to the generally accepted conditions of approval and disapproval between different points in the hierarchy and the way in which those affect people's behaviour and performance. Deserved recognition and praise may have a positive effect on the motivation of the recipient and vice versa.

Leibenstein sees the firm as a repository of information and experience; it therefore represents, in its entrepreneurial context, a growing facility to interpret changing conditions for the purposes of arbitrage and, by implication, profit.

THE 'NET' OF ECONOMIC INTERRELATIONSHIPS

Leibenstein attempts to clarify his vision of entrepreneurship by using the analogy of a net of pathways and nodes. In this analogy nodes refer to firms or households, and the inputs and outputs which flow between them move along the pathways. Given a condition of perfect competition, the net of nodes and pathways would be complete and well known. All actions and reactions would be catered for automatically without the requirement for judgements in order to realize abnormal profit. In reality, according to Leibenstein, there are both holes within the perceived net and many areas which are dark and unknown. Within the context of this theory, the traditional entrepreneurs or managerial entrepreneurs run the well-lit aspects of the net whereas the Schumpeterian entrepreneurs would work to light up the darker parts. The entrepreneur is the key figure in both economic growth and development by facilitating the further completion of the conceptual net.

One conclusion from this process is that the greater the level of competitive pressure the more of each individual entrepreneur's abilities will be utilized, and the more positively motivated will be the workforce within the structure and operation of the net or the economy, and therefore the faster its growth and development and the higher the level of x-efficiency.

Leibenstein goes on to develop this theory in the context of a demand and supply format: the demand for and supply of entrepreneurship.

The demand for entrepreneurship should be seen as a function of the number of gaps to be filled. The supply should be seen as a function of the cost of filling them, and also the quality and quantity of individuals with gap-filling or input-completing abilities as determined by a whole host of sociocultural factors. It is also related to the opportunity cost of becoming an entrepreneur, e.g. the possibility of sacrificing secure employment with a guaranteed income. Leibenstein indicates some of the potential shortfalls of this theory and derives the following conclusions as an indication of its relevance.

First, while the overall supply of individual entrepreneurs may be limiting, there remains the possibility of a surplus of some component skills: as it is the complete complement that distinguishes the individual entrepreneur. This reflects some of the observations made earlier from Say's work on the necessity for a complete set of characteristics in order to ensure successful entrepreneurship.

Second, Leibenstein highlights the need to reconsider investment criteria. He indicates the possibility of an unperceived reward from investments which although initially yielding a lower financial return on capital invested may release other entrepreneurial energies which traditional investment criteria do not accommodate in the calculation of overall return.

Third, he highlights the point that certain types of input may have detrimental side effects. As he describes it, 'input creation which would normally appear to be functional may in fact be disfunctional when the side effects are taken into account'. In this example he observes the possibility for the training of entrepreneurs to actually discourage entrepreneurship because of the opportunity cost involved in attending the courses designed to provide that training.

Fourth, he emphasizes the possibility of training for entrepreneurship.[5] While, as will be seen later, this may appear a contradiction in terms, it is important in that he refers it to those technical skills of entrepreneurship which are relevant to the co-ordination of factors of production in a traditional format, rather than in the creation of new products or production processes. This observation in a sense highlights the confusion which Leibenstein introduces into the theory of entrepreneurship by failing to apply his clear distinction between entrepreneurial activity as a source of economic change and entrepreneurial activity as a means of co-ordinating existing traditional techniques. The emphasis upon training should not be lost from an operational point of view, however, since many policy options refer precisely to this prospect of improving efficiency and effectiveness.

APPRAISAL

From the above summary of Leibenstein's theory of x-efficiency and his application of it to the theory of entrepreneurship, it is possible to identify certain important aspects from a positive viewpoint as well as certain significant shortcomings.

The major positive aspects which emerge from Leibenstein's theory refer first to the existence of a notion of inefficiency and lost output which may be attributed to a mismatch between the utility functions of the labour component of the commercial process. A further positive point emerges from the perceived ability to supplement skill patterns that enhance organizational performance.

So far as the output implications of different utility functions and their combination are concerned, the limiting case which this provides is significant in that it refers to a labour input with perfectly attuned objective utility functions. While this would appear ludicrous as a practical result it does identify one extreme on a continuum between perfect complementarity and, at the other extreme, perfect disunity. Clearly the operation of the labour input in different countries could be usefully considered within the context of this continuum. An obvious application of this approach would be in a comparative analysis of the motivational aspects of the labour forces in the UK vis-à-vis Japan. The recent incursions of Japanese management techniques into the British working environment highlight the potential for bringing the utility functions of individuals more directly into line with the interest of the company as a whole, by identifying individual interest with the overall company interest. It has further implications, however, for the ability of countries to take advantage of the perceived prospects of profit from arbitrage. This refers to the case, where the perception of arbitrage is realized by a number of different firms, or firms in different countries at the same time. Those firms which are most x-efficient because their labour input is both harmonious and motivated towards the effective production of nominal output will be able to realize or complete the arbitrage process first and therefore contain the apparent entrepreneurship. While this conclusion does not refer directly to Leibenstein's own work it emerges from it by extending the implications of his identification of x-efficiency and inefficiency.

In criticism of Leibenstein's contribution, his theory contains certain static elements which prohibit a clear perception of the dynamic role of entrepreneurship. His analogy of a net implies a relatively confined set of interrelationships between economic agents. This view is strengthened by his indication that Schumpeterian entrepreneurs light previously dark areas of the net, while other entrepreneurs repair it and generally improve performance within the well-lit sections. This approach distracts attention from the capacity of the net to change. Traditional production relationships may not be simply modified for greater efficiency; they may be completely changed such that the new pattern of inputs is unrecognizable from the old. It is important to acknowledge that entrepreneurial activity can, in certain cases, render classes of familiar economic activity redundant; effectively amputating whole sections of the well-lit net. The concept of a more or less well-mapped net denies the potential economic development discussed by Schumpeter since *changes* in its very structure and dimensions are precluded. If an analogy of this sort is considered desirable the number of pathways to each node engenders the notion of a multidimensional organic labyrinth rather than a net.

Acknowledging these criticisms, however, does not detract from the usefulness of the distinction which Leibenstein draws between entrepreneurial activity that principally relies upon a wholly new combination of resources and that which refines an existing combination. This distinction will be developed in the synthesis that follows.

REFERENCES

1. Leibenstein, H., 'Allocative efficiency v. "x-efficiency"', *American Economic Review*, **56**, 1966, pp. 392–415.
2. Stigler, G. J., 'The Xistence of x-efficiency', *American Economic Review*, **66**, 1976, pp. 213–16.
3. Ibid., p. 213.
4. Leibenstein, H., 'Entrepreneurship and development', *American Economic Review*, **58**, 1968, pp. 72–83.
5. Ibid.

CHAPTER
FOUR

TOWARDS A SYNTHESIS

If the word 'Swan' is to describe a bird that has the characteristic, among others, of appearing white, then those black birds in Australia must be called by another name, but if the criteria for being a swan are anatomical and do not mention colour, then the black and the white swans are in the same category. All the argument is about how to set up the categories, not the creatures. They are what they are however we choose to label them.[1]

INTRODUCTION

Some definitions and interpretations of entrepreneurship in an economic context have been considered in the preceding chapters. Although the term entrepreneur has been used in the English language for over two hundred years, there is not a consensus regarding the definition, characteristics or role of the entrepreneur. Superficially the situation could be taken to illustrate a confusion or conflict among those economists who have focused their attention on the subject. This is not the view taken here, however; the purpose of this chapter is to outline an interpretation of the situation that accepts major aspects of the contributions presented earlier as part of an overall picture that is consistent and complementary. The intention is to isolate subgroups of entrepreneurial activity that satisfy the definition presented towards the end of Chapter 1 and, simultaneously, satisfy the basic requirements for the interpretations put forward by the selected protagonists.

We identify three categories of entrepreneurial event: the *catalytic*, the *allocating*, and the *refining*. The last of these also includes the special case of entrepreneurial activity which can make a negative economic contribution, the *omega* event. The three key types are interrelated and essentially complementary in their interaction. We explain the main characteristics and sources of each along with their interreliance, prior to distilling their essential components to clarify their role for ease of comprehension given the frequent reference which is to be made to them in the remainder of the text.

NEW COMBINATIONS

The definition of an entrepreneurial event, presented at the end of Chapter 1, as 'an unrehearsed combination of economic resources instigated by the uncertain prospect of temporary monopoly profit', in one sense is adequate for the purpose of this chapter and is obviously related to the notion of 'new combinations of economic resources' used by Schumpeter. The idea of 'new' or 'unrehearsed' combinations provides a useful starting point for an economic theory of entrepreneurship. Immediately however, there appears the problem of establishing precisely what formally constitutes a 'new combination'.

The lack of homogeneity within categories of economic input is such that any combination of resources is likely to be different in one sense or another and probably 'new'. It could be that the attempted replication of a particular combination of economic resources is claimed to be new in the sense that there will necessarily be some differences between inputs that are accepted to be heterogeneous; land and labour epitomize the practical problems of differentiating a genuinely new combination.

Leibenstein explains part of substantial discrepancies in output per similar enterprise in terms of employees' attitudes and motivation. The significance of these factors is completely accepted here but Leibenstein's view could be extended to indicate that, as motivations and aspirations of individuals change through time, every day there is a new combination of human resources in a particular enterprise and thus a new combination of resources generally. In a sense this is correct: the distinction between the extreme interpretation of new combinations and entrepreneurial activity, however, is that the combination has not been 'instigated by the uncertain prospect of monopoly profit'. In other less extreme circumstances involving the establishment of a new business, for example, which has many inputs identical to those of an existing business and serving the same customer base with the same product, it can be genuinely problematic in practice to establish before the event whether or not the combination represents a genuinely new combination. Given that all other aspects of the entrepreneurial definition are satisfied, the establishment of a new business is not necessarily indicative of entrepreneurial activity. The entrepreneurial event, therefore, at a more pragmatic level, may require posthumous identification that relies upon the commercial effectiveness of the differentiating features.

CATEGORIES OF ENTREPRENEURIAL EVENT

Much of Schumpeter, Leibenstein, and the Austrians is accepted in connection with the role and description of entrepreneurial activity and events. Rather than take the differences between these contributors as indicators of the intractability of the subject matter, slightly amended, the different perspective and qualities ascribed to entreprencurial events as outlined in the earlier chapters can be taken to illustrate different species of a genus. As indicated towards the end of the Chapter 1, three subgroups are identified that can be expected to have different impacts on economic change and simultaneously be induced or constrained by different economic conditions. It is also accepted that entrepreneurial activity in one time-period determines the economic conditions that provide the context for entrepreneurial activity in the subsequent time-period and so on. Given this recursive system, there is the prospect for a mechanism that may describe self-perpetuating trends of economic activity that would be regarded as fluctuations or cycles.

THE SCHUMPETERIAN ENTREPRENEUR AND THE CATALYTIC EVENT

Schumpeter has provided the most complete description of a possible role for entrepreneurial events within an economy and specified particular characteristics of the entrepreneur. According to Schumpeter, the entrepreneur is not necessarily a capitalist and does not necessarily bear any risk in the event of the activity failing. Both of these propositions are refuted in Chapters 5 and 6. Schumpeter also maintains that an entrepreneurial event that is successful in a stationary economy is also successful because it has overcome the resistance of the economy's inertia. Once an event has been accommodated in the economy the way has been made easier for subsequent events so that a swarming of entrepreneurial activity can be anticipated. The interpretation offered here differs in so far as the distinguishing feature of the catalytic event is the uniqueness and lateral thought embodied in the development and not the success of overcoming an economy's resistance. The combination of resources assembled in this initial catalytic event does not represent a gradualistic progression from existing commercial operations but something that is fundamentally new which can redirect the focus and activity of others working on the refinement and adaptation of existing processes, products, designs, and services. The commercial application can not be traced back in incremental steps to the proceeding state of the art. There has been a commercial metamorphosis.

A key feature of the 'new combinations' described by Schumpeter is that the innovation of an entrepreneurial event has a positive impact on the position of the economy's production possibility frontier: 'we will simply define innovation as the setting up of a new production function'.[2]

This is accepted and is central to what follows: the catalytic event introduces the potential for further entrepreneurial activity into an economy but it is not accepted that this potential is automatically realized by a swarm of similar entrepreneurs. Rather it is suggested that the potential may, or may not, be realized: in the case where the potential is exploited, this may be achieved with relative speed by a different category of entrepreneurial event.

THE AUSTRIAN ENTREPRENEUR AND THE ALLOCATING EVENT

For those economists of the Austrian School, an economy will never achieve a steady-state equilibrium. There will be continually appearing opportunities for entrepreneurial activity. New combinations of resources will be arranged that are calculated to fill emerging market gaps and provide temporary monopoly profits. In the ordinary course of a dynamic economy this category of activity will be occurring: competition would quite swiftly erode the profits and begin a gravitation towards an existing production possibility frontier. Equilibrium would not be achieved by the activity of these allocating events but they would act to move an overall allocation in the direction of an ever-moving target on a given frontier. Clearly in the scheme that is being developed here, the occurrence of a catalytic event would create many market gaps that appear simultaneously—a swarm or frenzy of activity in the form of allocating events, which can be clearly distinguished from the catalytic event by virtue of the fact that the commercial origins of the allocating event *can* be traced back to previous developments. An example would be a modified or new application of the principle introduced by a particular catalytic event.

LEIBENSTEIN'S ENTREPRENEUR AND THE REFINING EVENT

As indicated above Leibenstein's role for the entrepreneur emerged from his work on x-efficiency and developed into the identification of two distinct entrepreneurial types.

From Leibenstein's perspective it was conceivable that the allocation of resources within an economy could be the best attainable but, for that optimal allocation, there could still remain inefficiency in terms of the input and output of resources. It is important to distinguish the resource-use efficiency with which Leibenstein was concerned from the allocative efficiency of the classicists and neo-classicists. According to these schools of thought the economic efficiency achieved at equilibrium is an allocational efficiency in so far as there is not an alternative allocation of resources that could be arranged without reducing the utility of at least one individual in the economy—for the given distribution of income. Resource-use inefficiency would provide the economic incentive for an entrepreneur. By reducing or removing resourse-use inefficiency, either a greater output for a given input or a constant output for a reduced input is possible. Either outcome, or an intermediary position, would imply a profit. It is for this type of activity in particular that the practical problems of isolating a 'new combination', discussed earlier, would be most severe.

If Leibenstein's interpretation is accepted then an economy could be in equilibrium while there is also an incentive for entrepreneurial activity. Under such circumstances entrepreneurial activity could spontaneously appear. Successfully realized, the activity would push the economy's imperfect equilibrium nearer to the production possibility frontier but never beyond it. In a dynamic economy, that is one that is continually readjusting, some firms and industries will be adversely affected. An immediate and rational response for those firms affected would be to remove x-inefficiency where possible. There would be a negative stimulus for entrepreneurial activity and refined events in depressed industries, sectors, or regions.

A SPECIAL CASE—THE OMEGA EVENT

In a dynamic economy different sectors and industries will at times be buoyant and at times depressed. Certain industries and firms will be adversely affected in the course of economic restructuring and will ultimately shed labour and plant as part of, or as a prelude to, the liquidation process. The labour, which can originate from all levels of personnel, will have a collection of skills and experiences that have become redundant. The opportunity cost of this labour will be low, possibly zero. Similarly, the opportunity cost of the plant and machinery being disposed of from these industries will be low. This situation is temporary, it reflects restructuring, and only arises because a real economy experiences time lags, imperfect information and significant investments in human capital that the proprietors are reluctant, or unable, to write off. In this situation it could be that the labour and plant released from declining industries could recombine in genuinely 'new combinations' as they have been defined here, to operate as new firms in the short term.

Omega activity is not seen as a separate category of entrepreneurial activity; rather it is taken to be an extreme and special form of the refining event: it will ordinarily reflect a negative stimulus in a particular industry or sector or be associated with limited employment alternatives.

STEADY-STATE EQUILIBRIUM AND THE CIRCULAR FLOW

The idea of a steady-state equilibrium is a useful distraction in so far as it provides a clear and uncluttered starting point from which to consider the possible affects of entrepreneurial activity. Whether the equilibrium is that of the circular flow of economic life or the classical circular flow of income is not relevant here. An economic order is known and accepted. Without there being some change of data that defines the position, the equilibrium will be maintained in perpetuity. Here, we consider two routes by which the data may change. The first of these could be described as a shock: that is a significant, unanticipated change of data that dislocates the existing equilibrium. The second may be in the form of a pressure that requires marginal adjustment from a macro perspective. A shock could be construed as a shift of the economy's production possibility frontier and contrasted with a pressure that would involve movement along or towards the production possibility frontier. In the absence of either a shock or pressure there is no requirement, or possibility, for 'new combinations': there would be no entrepreneurial activity. The concept of equilibria is the focus of analysis for the classicists and considered implausible by the Austrians; for Leibenstein there could be x-efficiency at an equilibrium but no attempt to remove it. Schumpeter takes equilibrium as the starting point for his analysis.

Shocks to the economic system may either be endogenous or exogenous. Endogenous shocks would include the first commercial application of a new technology or the commercial appearance of an approach or combination of resources that has ramifications and applications elsewhere within the economy. The endogenous shock is the outcome of entrepreneurial activity according to Schumpeter and, by the definitions he has used, there can only be a positive impact on the position of the economy's production possibility frontier. The appearance of a catalytic entrepreneurial event that constitutes an endogenous shock yields for the instigator a temporary monopoly profit. More significant than this profit, however, is the potential it creates for refined and redirected applications throughout other sectors of the economy. For the potential of a catalytic event to be realized requires a complement of Austrian-type entrepreneurial activity. It is important to recognize that the full impact of a catalytic event, brought about by Schumpeterian activity, is dependent upon the execution of allocating events. There is no automatic mechanism for the allocating events to occur, however; the potential for profit has been introduced but it need not be exploited. Certainly the rate at which the potential is exploited is indeterminate.

Catalytic and allocating activity would constitute economic development and be consistent with industrial restructuring. In turn there would be industries and sectors adversely affected by the development path and a negative stimulus for the appearance of refining events prompted by the need to remove x-inefficiency.

Omega events may be stimulated in particularly depressed sectors that are releasing resources with no alternative employment opportunities.

Exogenous shocks to the economy would include acts of God, war and other major disruptions that occur outside the economic system but still have an impact upon the economy. An exogenous shock can present market opportunities after the event that had not previously existed. The opportunities will be exploited by allocating entrepreneurial activity in the same way as if the opportunities had arisen from an endogenous shock. The implications of an exogenous shock, however, may be positive or negative in terms of the emerging production possibility frontier: where the new frontier lies within the preceding frontier, the adjustment process, when complete and perfectly executed, produces an equilibrium associated with a lower level of national welfare. This result is clearly reversed if the shock has a positive impact. It is important to recognize that an exogenous shock can provide the opportunity, or potential, for allocating activity that stimulates refining and possibly, omega activity as before, but there are no implications for the catalytic entrepreneurial activity perceived by Schumpeter.

ECONOMIC PRESSURES

These may be exogenous or endogenous and could include gradual climatic changes, demographic movements, changing patterns of consumer preference and income, etc. Economic data would be evolving and a gradual reallocation of resources is both desirable and viable. The pressure may be discharged as gradually as it accumulates if reallocation between existing combinations is a feasible and adequate response. Alternatively this pressure may be discharged with the introduction of a 'new combination'. A market gap appears and is susceptible to exploitation by allocating activity. The allocating activity moves the economy relatively quickly towards a new equilibrium on the production possibility frontier. The potential for development, however, will be restricted by the same boundary as before. The critical function for the allocator is to identify accurately when the pressure has achieved a level that would allow the event to be viable. If the event is premature it will not be viable, while if the event is delayed there becomes the prospect of the potential profit being appropriated by another operator.

The significance of allocating and refining events from a development perspective is only that they determine the speed and efficiency with which a new equilibrium is approached. The production possibility frontier is not affected by these activities. During the adjustment process there will be inefficiency and either a reduced level of welfare or an additional requirement for resources to achieve a given level of welfare. From a governmental perspective, disequilibrium would be attractive in so far as the apparent activity of adjustment would reflect favourably on national statistics, particularly if there were unemployed resources before the readjustment. Satisfaction with manipulated disequilibrium or continuous adjustment to exogenous pressures would clearly be myopic except for beneficial multiplier affects. Similarly, entrepreneurial activity of the sort envisaged by Schumpeter is not necessarily important: the potential for extra consumption is only valued if a mechanism exists to realize that potential. Adopting these different categories of entrepreneurial activity, and acknowledging the conditions necessary for their appearance and impact, allows us to anticipate very little of the economy from generally observing the level of *apparent* entrepreneurial activity. On the one hand the occurrence of entrepreneurial events could reflect an economy in disequilibrium that is in the process of adjustment but that will not be 'better-off' than when it was at a preceding equilibrium: while on the other hand the non-existence of apparent activity could reflect a satisfactory approximation to an equilibrium where 'new combinations' can only be introduced at the expense of some consumer's utility.

ENTREPRENEURIAL ACTIVITY IN AN OPEN ECONOMY

If the mechanisms suggested are accepted then it is easily argued that the level of entrepreneurial activity itself is not important. More important is the rate at which the different types of event occur.

If the entrepreneurial activity comprises catalytic events exclusively then the development of an economy may be imperceptible because there is no follow-up innovation via allocation events. Under these conditions, the potential which the catalyst provides is not taken up in the economy of origin due to a failure by others to recognize the potential for arbitrage which has been created. It might be realized in other economies, however, and the advantages conveyed may rebound on the economy of origin through the trade balance. Subsequent refinements may occur due to the impact of increased competition from imports, the source of which are the allocation events in other economies. There may, however, be a proliferation of omega recycling of obsolete plant and equipment, and skills, with the associated negative impact upon the speed of development. This would be ironic, in some senses, given that the catalytic event originated in the economy concerned.

If the entrepreneurial activity is devoid of catalytic events then development and positive economic change is only possible either through exogenous shocks which carry with them at least an equal possibility of inducing negative economic change, or imported information from catalytic events in other economies. Unless such foreign catalytic events are accompanied by a lack of allocating events in the economy of origin then the time-lags involved may preclude successful allocation in the domestic economy prior to import penetration.

If the frequency with which catalytic events are enacted is high in relation to the appearance of allocating events the full potential will not be achieved throughout the economy before subsequent catalytic events redirect the focus of allocating activity. In the limiting case where there is no 'friction' of adjustment, this need not be a problem. In fact friction does exist and the allocating activity could be rendered fruitless by subsequent events, or less fruitful in so far as only the realized allocating events would contribute to development. The allocating activity pursued but not completed would be lost.

If the appearance of catalytic events is infrequent in relation to the allocating entrepreneurial activity there will be diminishing marginal returns for the allocating endeavour and, ultimately, a hiatus and gravitation towards an equilibrium in the absence of exogenous shocks. The profits of arbitrage for allocating events will swiftly be reduced to zero.

Irrespective of the stimulus that has prompted allocating activity there will be adverse affects experienced by specific industries and firms. It is in these firms that the stimulus for refined activity will determine in part the speed with which existing, established businesses disappear from the economy and the rate with which resources are released from these affected industries for redeployment and potential omega activity.

For a domestic economy freely trading on international markets the catalytic events can be imported and exploited by indigenous allocating activity: conversely a catalytic event appearing domestically can be exploited by trading partners. It is the speed of execution that determines the duration and total value of the temporary monopoly profits. If the allocating entrepreneurial events are more swiftly perceived and enacted in foreign economies, domestic allocating events can only work to ensure that the monopoly profits are shorter lived than otherwise. In the case of allocating activity, the uncertainty is compounded: the market size is imprecisely known for an innovation but also the timing of a competitors' appearance is unknown. This latter consideration could determine the viability of a planned allocating event and simultaneously represent an inefficient temporary deployment of resources. In the case where a characteristic of the domestic economy is for the allocating entrepreneurial activity to emerge after foreign activity, the outcome could be more detrimental than if there were to be no domestic response. Domestic allocating activities can only work to reduce profit: the financial criteria for the realization of allocating events will not alter but the anticipated returns will.

The above examples of potential mismatches in the incidence of different entrepreneurial types are just a few of the many possible permutations which can be envisaged. The introduction of the prospect of imported and exported catalytic and allocating events serves to complicate the picture further. The overriding observation which emerges, however, is analogous to those made by Say when considering the requirements of successful entrepreneurship, and echoed by Leibenstein in his notion of input completion. The full developmental impact of entrepreneurship can only be obtained via the requisite balance in the incidence of the three types of event which have been presented.

Catalytic events require allocating events for their further dissemination. The adjustment problems presented require refining events to ensure that those industries affected maximize the efficiency with which their own inputs are used. Under 'perfect' conditions, the adjustment process will be completed in the absence of unnecessary costs because the restructuring process is accompanied by heightened efficiency in declining industries to ensure that only the appropriate level of factor allocations is still made to them. Omega activity would tend not to occur because allocating and refining events absorb and reintegrate available labour. As indicated, such perfection is unlikely, if not impossible. Comparative advantage will reside in those economies where it is closest.

The main problem which this new input completion requirement introduces derives from the variation in the balance between the different types of entrepreneurial event which would be expected to prevail in practice. Different kinds of catalytic event would have different allocation and refining implications. Since catalytic events are, by definition, unpredictable, it is impossible to anticipate their allocation and refining requirements for 'perfect' adjustment.

Comparative advantage will therefore reside within those economies which have greater flexibility in allocating and refining responses. This requires, in turn, a favourable access to the information necessary for such enterprises to be undertaken with confidence. Some of these informational aspects are considered further in the penultimate chapter of the text. The preceding arguments are sufficient to illustrate how the delineation of various entrepreneurial events is crucial to determining the economic contribution of entrepreneurship, but also how complex and subtle are the interrelationships which emerge.

CONCLUSION

In this chapter an attempt has been made to isolate categories of entrepreneurial activity that have distinguishable roles within the economy. The argument suggests that entrepreneurial activity is not a sufficient condition for economic development, although economic development will not occur without entrepreneurial activity. Three subgroups have been identified that acknowledge the generic nature of entrepreneurship: the subgroups are heavily based upon the contributions of Schumpeter, the Austrians, and Leibenstein. The crucial feature for economic development is that the distinguished event-types are consequential and complementary. A deficiency in a specific type of entrepreneurial event will have implications for economic performance that will not necessarily be overcome by the proliferation of those activity-types already present. Furthermore, it can be anticipated that the constraints and impediments faced by the instigators of even the isolated categories of events will differ and policy intervention will be more effective if it is tailored to achieve a particular outcome. A prerequisite for this relatively sophisticated policy approach is to identify those constraints that are pertinent and significant to particular types of entrepreneurial event. Part Two attempts this by an examination of the factor markets faced by the instigators of new combinations.

Much of what follows involves analyses which focus upon the differential contribution of the entrepreneurial types identified. Given the frequent and comparative usage of references to each it is important to retain a clear understanding of their main characteristics, otherwise the significance of the arguments will be lost. To facilitate this retention we have decided to label each type in a way which serves as a reminder of their different roles. This strategy is not without risk, however, since, from the preceding arguments, it is abundantly clear that no single title can convey fully the specific contributions associated with each type. The category labels should therefore be treated as indicative reminders rather than definitive labels which unambiguously encapsulate the nature of each kind of entrepreneur. These titles have already been used above and can be summarized as follows:

1. *The catalytic entrepreneurial event or activity* refers to the pure Schumpeterian concept with the modifications explained earlier and to be expanded upon in subsequent chapters. These represent the first or unique innovation of a new combination. Its subsequent impact on the economy will be determined by the extent of subsequent innovation by our second category.
2. *The allocating event or activity* refers to the wave of subsequent innovation as the catalytic event becomes acknowledged within the circular flow. In the process of reallocation there will be casualties and increased competition for shrinking markets in some areas of the circular flow. This will provoke entrepreneurial activity of the third kind.
3. *The refining event or activity* reflects the need for firms to improve the effectiveness of their existing pattern of resource usage in the face of altered competition. A special case within this category is that of the omega event, where resources released are often available at abnormally low cost to be 'recycled' for a short period of time by a new owner-manager.

The dynamic implications of these categories in the process of economic development are considered in Part Two below.

REFERENCES

1. Robinson, J., *Economic Philosophy*, Penguin, London, 1964, p. 8.
2. Schumpeter, J. A., *Business Cycles: A Theoretical Historical and Statistical Analysis of the Capitalist Process*, 1st edn, 2nd impression, McGraw-Hill, Maidenhead, 1939.

PART
TWO

FACTOR MARKET ANALYSIS

INTRODUCTION TO PART TWO

Part One reviewed competing views of the economic role for entre-preneurship. Although there are many striking differences between the views of the selected contributors, a common, but surrogate feature of the work considered, was the preoccupation with the impact of entrepreneurial events upon economic conditions. In Part Two the main objective is to examine the occurrence and role of entrepreneurship within a dynamic context, accom-modating the impact of an economic condition upon entrepreneurial activity. This can be seen as the second part of a recursive system which considers the influence of entrepreneurial activity upon economic development and the influence of economic development upon entrepreneurship. It could be assumed, for example, that an economy which is constantly changing due to the successful realization of entrepreneurial events would facilitate imagin-ative and unconstrained thinking, less contextual inertia and a greater propensity for further entrepreneurial activity. This would be comparable with the notion of a self-perpetuating entrepreneurial function, an 'enterprise culture' fuelling economic development with a stream of efficiently exploited discrete changes.

An additional recursive process could also be influential and would be a purely economic one. It is on the components of this system that Part Two focuses.

Entrepreneurial events displace the prevailing pattern of factor allocation. Simultaneously entrepreneurial activity creates and adjusts to a revised pattern of resource allocation and provides the stimulus and context for subsequent activity. The important point which factor market analysis emphasizes is the extent to which relative qualities, characteristics, and prices obtaining in factor markets determine the ensuing pattern of realized entrepreneurship. Conditions in factor markets determine which of the stock of entrepreneurial visions held within an economy at any one time will appear viable and worthy of pursuing further.

The importance of making a clear distinction between categories of entrepreneurial event emerges clearly from the nature of this recursive system. The nature of economic development reflects the prevalence of particular types of entrepreneurial activity. Catalytic and allocating events cause economic development by creating new combinations which expand the potential of the economy or realize unexploited potential. Refining and omega events enable a more effective or expedient revision to existing combinations.

Factor market analysis attempts to assess in a very general way, the relative probability of the categories of entrepreneurial event occurring and their impact upon subsequent economic change. Any economic change will comprise discrete and evolutionary movements. From a policy perspective, naïve attempts to increase the amount of entrepreneurial activity in a recession, for example, may not influence the number of catalytic and allocation events but may stimulate the appearance of refining and omega events. With crude proxies for entrepreneurial activity such as the number of new company registrations, for example, the policy may be seen as successful although the impact on economic change has been negligible.

The profile and mix of entrepreneurial events will vary according to the economic conditions in specific industries, regions, or the national economy. The implications for policy will therefore differ according to the relative level and rate of change of economic activity at a disaggregated level.

Factor-market analysis refers to the impact of changes in the circular flow upon the different factor markets confronting potential instigators of entrepreneurial activity. In the context of policy design the main focus for the economist is the mechanism by which factor markets respond to changes in economic conditions and the extent to which policy can encourage smooth and efficient adjustment in different industries, regions, and the economy as a whole.

Despite the dynamic context in which Schumpeter's theory rests, the unidirectional element of causality between entrepreneurial events and economic change means that the theory does not accommodate the impact of economic change upon the timing and realization of subsequent entrepreneurial activity. It is clear, however, that many aspects of factor-market behaviour stem from time-lags: the adjustment process is not instantaneous, as assumed by the classicists and neo-classicists. The time-lags can reflect very practical considerations, for example the construction and installation time of new plant designed to exploit a market opportunity. Alternatively, the time-lags may reflect less tangible inertia that becomes more entrenched as methods and protocol become institutionalized. The skill pattern of a labour force, for example, may become rigid and immutable over time as work practices and training/education procedures formalize and concretize; as individuals become familiar with one way of operating there will become a natural reluctance to formulate, learn, refine, and adopt new systems. The longer the status quo is maintained, the greater the inertia becomes, reflecting the physical and human investment in the systems developed for requirements originally identified.

Financial institutions, the design and use of premises, the nature of the education process, will all reflect different levels of rigidity according to the degree of stability in the circular flow and the length of time for which it has prevailed. The pattern of resistance to entrepreneurial events is more sensibly described in terms of the various factor markets rather than simply as a vague notion of resistance to change. The entrepreneurial events which disturb an equilibrium and overcome the pattern of resistance may tend to occur in sectors and regions where the prevailing inertia in the relevant factor markets is least established. Some entrepreneurial actions which would have been viable with one pattern of factor conditions would be unviable with another.

The dynamic process is only complete if this recursive framework is acknowleged. Entrepreneurial activity will cause changes in economic structure and, therefore, in the pattern of factor markets and their future resistance to subsequent entrepreneurial events.

Entrepreneurial events realized in any economy do not reflect the full stock of events that could have occurred under different market conditions. The direction of economic development therefore incorporates a random or stochastic element which is not determined by superficial policy design. It is unhelpful to attempt to predict entrepreneurial events: it is however possible to predict the way imperfections and particular characteristics of individual factor markets will impinge on categories of entrepreneurial event. This approach facilitates a theory of entrepreneurship which incorporates the causal linkages between entrepreneurial events and economic change and between economic change and entrepreneurial events.

Part Two approaches factor-market analysis by accepting three basic assumptions, they are:

1. Human capital is one key element in any conceived and attempted entrepreneurial activity. This can be manifested in one of the three main categories of entrepreneurial event discussed in the final chapter of Part One.
2. Financial capital is a complementary and crucial element in any entrepreneurial activity. This can be used to acquire at least temporary control over any one, or combination, of three categories of economic resource. These are usually described as land, labour including intellectual property, and capital that will be referred to here as plant and machinery to keep clear the distinction between financial and physical capital.
3. The condition of the economy will be determined by, and in part determine, the level and nature of entrepreneurial activity.

To achieve the objective of this section there are four chapters. The first three chapters consider the generic factor markets of entrepreneurship, finance, and secondary inputs. The treatment is necessarily brief and excludes much of the minutiae which could easily justify dedicated texts. Instead, these chapters attempt to highlight the features and peculiarities of individual factor markets that would constitute constraints upon the perceived level of entrepreneurial activity. Simultaneously, these features can be seen to be dynamic themselves, inducing or prohibiting entrepreneurship in a predictable way. These chapters investigate the conditions which confront potential entrepreneurial activity and discuss, on *a priori* grounds, the anticipated propensity for categories of entrepreneurial event to be realized under different conditions. The fundamental components of any business activity, and entrepreneurial activity in particular, are human capital and financial capital; these are considered separately under generalized macroeconomic conditions. The factor markets for plant and machinery, labour, and premises are considered under the umbrella of secondary inputs. This reflects the implicit assumption that with adequate finance, constraints emanating from these markets could more or less easily be overcome. There will be many weaknesses with such a generalized overview of the economic condition: in particular an economy that is static in terms of GDP and employment figures may be experiencing major restructuring with buoyant and declining industries working to compensate each other. Similarly, regional disparities may be significant but compensating when put into a national context. There will be numerous legitimate caveats to be introduced in any particular circumstance but for the purpose of this discussion they will be omitted rather than extend and complicate what in essence is a straight-forward approach that could be tailored to suit particular situations and requirements.

FIVE

THE FACTOR MARKET FOR ENTREPRENEURSHIP

INTRODUCTION

In view of the emphasis placed on the entrepreneurial event in the preceding chapters and the economic categories of entrepreneurial event which have been identified to satisfy the definition presented in Chapter 1, it is necessary to highlight explicitly a convenience that is made in the following discussion of entrepreneurship. The entrepreneur, it was argued, is a title applied to the conceptual construct and could not be used to categorize individuals: rather it was suggested that the qualities of the entrepreneur were in fact more likely to be transitory and fluid, being exhibited according to the context, and perceived stimuli. In this chapter, for ease of presentation, but without rejecting either of the tenets presented above, the term entrepreneur will be used to describe the pending or actual person or group instigating an entrepreneurial event. For the purposes of examining the factor market of entrepreneurship it is convenient to refer to entrepreneurs although these may be individuals working in isolation or in informal groups or they may be more formalized groups employed within an existing commercial organization.

A discussion of the psychological characteristics and motivations of entrepreneurs is beyond the scope of this work, and more useful insights are likely to come from disciplines other than economics. Nevertheless, it must be acknowledged that an economic situation which is believed to be deficient in entrepreneurial activity cannot be taken to imply that there is necessarily a shortage of entrepreneurs. The stock of potential entrepreneurs may be high but their activity could be suppressed by facets of the economic, political, or social systems which impede entrepreneurial activity. Clearly there is a major difference between policy that is engineered to remove constraints upon potential entrepreneurial activity and policy that is designed to produce more entrepreneurs.

In this chapter an attempt is made to consider the conditions and impediments that might impinge on a potential entrepreneur and that, if severe enough, could reduce the number of entrepreneurial events realized.

PRELIMINARY CONSIDERATIONS

The definition of an entrepreneurial event offered earlier is our starting point: in Chapter 1, an entrepreneurial event was defined as 'an unrehearsed combination of economic resources instigated by the uncertain prospect of temporary-monopoly profit'.

From this definition there are four areas to focus upon. Considering the components of the definition there is first the unrehearsed or new allocation of resources. For a new allocation to be conceived and orchestrated there requires to be imagination and knowledge available to the instigator and the freedom or latitude to investigate the implications of the idea. For the idea to be progressed to an unrehearsed allocation of economic resources requires that factor markets are flexible enough to allow resources to be diverted from their existing uses. Impediments to the flow and acquisition of knowledge or conditions that inhibit imaginative combinations will restrict entre-preneurship. Similarly constraints upon the flow of resources will restrict enacted entrepreneurship.

The remaining component of our definition highlights the other three areas of focus: 'the uncertain prospect of temporary-monopoly profit'.

Without having to align the argument with the assumption of profit maximization, the prospect of profit will be required for the event to be distinguished from pure research, from non-commercial folly and to com-pensate the possibility of financial loss.

Characteristics of the context in which entrepreneurs operate that affect either the magnitude of uncertainty or profit will have bearings upon the apparent quantity of entrepreneurial activity and, at the margin, determine which potential entrepreneurial events are actually realized.

It also needs to be explicitly acknowledged that the ownership of residual profit, or entrepreneurial profit, is likely to be more significant than the enterprises' profit *per se*. If, for example, the claims on an enterprise's profit, that is the profit from the successful realization of a particular entrepreneur-ial event, are in proportion to the finance invested in shares and that a substantial portion of the shares are secured by financiers, be they a parent or employing organization or commercial investor, the profit available to the entrepreneur concerned may be inadequate despite a return on capital employed that is attractive enough to engender external participation.

The final area of focus is the most problematic: the entrepreneurial profit, in Schumpeter's tradition, is expected to be temporary. The profit is eroded as the demand for the product, process, or service is satisfied by competitors who establish themselves to offer similar or refined output. Effective and unrestrained competition is at the heart of the neo-classical explanation for efficiency in terms of resource allocation. Monopoly is an imperfection in the competitive ideal and is demonstrated to provide restricted output at inflated prices: effective policy to remove monopoly in every shape or form would remove the principal motive accepted here for entrepreneurial endeavour. The conditions which determine the effective time horizon of the entrepreneurs' temporary profits will be significant. It might be argued that a consideration of those factors which influence the duration of entrepreneurial profit is little more than a red herring in so far as the profit referred to earlier must refer to the capitalized value of any profit stream and that given a time horizon and an appropriate discount rate any discussion is completely confined to those entrepreneurial events with adequate positive net present values. The point that is to be considered here revolves around the fact that neither the time horizon nor the discount rate are 'given' and both are subject to influences from outside the economic system.

As with our discussion of the categories of entrepreneurial event, so it is useful to retain and reiterate four types of entrepreneur that relate to the categories of events.

The catalytic entrepreneur represents the purveyor of Schumpeterian entrepreneurial events in neat form. This refers to individuals who provide entrepreneurial actions of such fundamental force that they displace the equilibrium in the circular flow as defined by Schumpeter and discussed in Chapter 4.

The allocating entrepreneur is more like that depicted by Cantillon and the Austrians. The entrepreneur is alert to potential arbitrage, to market gaps and to emerging patterns of demand. Major opportunities may become available to allocating entrepreneurs following a catalytic event but the converse is not the case and subsequent catalytic activity is only affected in so far as allocating activity in part determines the context into which a catalytic event must fit.

The refining entrepreneur is evoked in Leibenstein's discussion of x-efficiency as the entrepreneur who anticipates deriving a profit from improved organizational efficiency applied to an existing allocation of resources. The new combination of resources that results from such an innovative revision of an existing combination may be major within the micro context in which it is orchestrated, but is incapable of inter-industry application in the schema presented here. Where the revision does have inter-industry applications and increases the potential output of an operation rather than increasing the output achieved, the status of the entrepreneur would be more correctly that of the catalytic type and there would be implications for an outward shift of the production possibility frontier.

The final category of entrepreneur is the omega entrepreneur: this individual is a subgroup of the refining entrepreneur and is a temporary entrepreneur in so far as the initial viability, or quasi viability, of the business is derived from low, post-disturbance costs. The entrepreneurial event engineered by this individual is the most evident outcome of restructuring and, without further entrepreneurial input, will not gravitate to a place within any equilibrium or circular flow.

Having identified and presented four groups of entrepreneurs as distinct entities it is important to stress that as the entrepreneur can include an individual ploughing a lone furrow, a group of individuals working independently of any business organization, or an existing commercial organization, so it is that subgroups of the genus entrepreneur can not be definitely isolated in reality. The four groups can more usefully be thought of as stereotypes on a continuum. In any observable case there may be dispute as to which category is most appropriate for an entrepreneur: the entrepreneur may be more or less of the catalytic type with overtones of the allocating type, or vice versa, but there could not be confusion between non-adjacent groupings.

Common to all categories of entrepreneur, however, is a requirement for an understanding of business. Precisely what should constitute that understanding would be determined by the type of entrepreneurial event envisaged, although a common core could be defined. It is only noted in passing that the opportunity to acquire the common core is rarely available as part of the orthodox education provision and that those professional qualifications relating to business are characterized by a particular functional or subject slant. Everything else being held equal, the provision of such basic education would facilitate, if not increase, the amount of entrepreneurship within an economy. The nature of constraints upon entrepreneurs are most clearly explained by considering each type in turn.

THE CATALYTIC ENTREPRENEUR

This entrepreneur pursues an event that represents a genuinely and completely new combination of resources. It can not be traced back to a similar commercial innovation in another part of the economy: it embodies a new insight that probably reflects an accumulation of knowledge combined with imagination producing a catastrophic, spontaneous event. Somewhere there has been lateral thought or a discrete jump of conceptualization. The catalytic entrepreneur accepts the task of presenting the ensuing product or service to market: the underlying idea is not necessarily the entrepreneur's, but for the motivation to be strongest and therefore the likelihood of success to be greatest, it is helpful if the entrepreneur becomes a surrogate parent of the idea.

Precisely why or when the embryonic insight is achieved is impossible to comment upon. It might be supposed that an increased rate of data collection, interpretation, and dissemination would increase the likelihood of such events occurring although it need not be the case, and a retardation in these processes may provoke a productive reconsideration of information that has been available for a long time. For the data to be reviewed in a positive and unconventional manner may require a faculty that can be strengthened by particular attitudinal approaches to education and employment. On the other hand, rigid, unfashionable approaches to education and employment may engender precisely the required facility by promoting rebellion. It is beyond the scope of this text to investigate these issues; rather it is simply accepted that they happen in a random way.

It is important to recognize, however, that the entrepreneurial vision, which is little more than an individual's dream, is not the entrepreneurial event complete and the gestation period required to transform the vision into a saleable item with an estimated effective demand may range from a few months to many years depending on the nature of the event. The longer the gestation period the greater the uncertainty that profits will be available and, everything else being equal, the greater the initial costs incurred with the project.

One immediately striking feature of this situation is the large range of skills required by the entrepreneur during the gestation period. On the one hand is the case where the entrepreneur performs or oversees all the functions personally and therefore must be adept at product/service prototype design, supply and contract organization, market research, operational strategies, financial analysis and management, personnel specification, and recruitment, etc. Even were it conceivable to find an individual with a complete range of the requisite specialized technical and commercial skills, the time required to complete all of the tasks involved would be substantial and requires a financial independence that would only be available to a portion of the population with significant sums accumulated in previous periods.

There is a trade-off between the time taken during the gestation period and the expense of engaging specialists to undertake components of the overall task. Employing third-party specialists has three major drawbacks. First there is the substantial expense involved in employing these people. Second there is the risk that the concept will be stolen and exploited by third parties and finally, there is the problem of assessing the competence of the specialists.

An accurate assessment of the costs and hurdles to be faced during the gestation period of the more ambitious catalytic type event would be daunting to any ordinary individual and a major deterrent to an informal entrepreneurial group. It also has to be stressed that much of the time and expense referred to would be incurred before the initial idea could be presented to financial backers. The briefest consideration of the processes and expenses involved would suggest that catalytic events would more realistically be pursued by entrepreneurs within existing organizations where there would be easier access to the required networks, a wider base of knowledge and experience, and where the initial funds could be more accessible.

The implications of these superficial observations are quite major in so far as the catalytic type event and the entrepreneur who pursues the event does not fit comfortably into any conventional scenario. On the one hand the expense of refining an entrepreneurial vision to the point that external investors can be approached may well be prohibitively expensive for the individual or private group, while on the other hand an organization that performs its current commercial operations efficiently is unlikely to have the spare capacity to follow up on catalytic visions as they appear. Furthermore, the organization's structure will be critical to the realization of events and in some cases will be unable to receive and accommodate ideas. There would be a big difference between acknowledging and accepting suggestions to improve current operations and actually innovating those which have major strategic implications for the reorganization of inputs.

It is difficult to see how catalytic events are actually realized. There is no established market for the vision and severe obstacles for the individual or employed entrepreneur. Nevertheless, experience shows that some catalytic entrepreneurial events do survive the gestation period.

It is pertinent to observe that the lateral thought or conceptualization that produces the catalytic entrepreneurial vision is assumed here to be a random event but the speed with which the vision is worked on, either by private individuals or employees of an existing organization, can be varied according to the perceived urgency associated with the entrepreneurial event. A vision that has been worked on to the point that there could be a product or service ready for sale may be held back for strategic reasons. Thus the appearance of the vision may be uncontrolled but the rate of development can be more or less closely controlled as can the launch be timed to suit wider considerations.

This raises a further facet to the opening question which related to the problem of establishing whether there was a shortage of entrepreneurs or a shortage of entrepreneurial events reflecting impediments to their realization. The additional facet raises the possibility of a situation arising where there are adequate entrepreneurs, no effective barriers to entrepreneurship, but entrepreneurial events being strategically withheld in anticipation of a particularly opportune time when each event will have a larger impact in terms of profit or profile.

RESISTANCE AND THE IMPACT ON CATALYTIC ACTIVITY

The entrepreneur, by the definitions we are using here, pursues an unconventional allocation of resources. The resistance, in terms of aversion to the unknown, that this entrepreneur encounters will be greater than that faced by lower-order entrepreneurs. The potential significance of the catalytic event is also greater than the other forms of entrepreneurial event.

There are strong reasons to suppose that an economy which is prosperous and buoyant will have characteristics that are more conducive to the appearance of catalytic events. With reference to the resistance faced by the entrepreneur, it is assumed that the innovation of a new idea can come from three principal sources.

First there is the resistance from potential financiers who may be more cautious when the industry concerned, or the entire economy, is in recession or depressed. On the one hand they will be influenced by business closures or contractions, while on the other, they will be aware of the depressed demand for their funds. Any risk associated with the entrepreneurial event will be perceived to be greater in such conditions. The portfolio of new investments will be smaller in depressed conditions and the influence of catalytic failure will be proportionately greater than in more prosperous times when the size of funds invested is large, and the spread of investments is wide.

The second source of resistance may emanate from the intended consumers of the new product, process, or service. In recession, certain consumers will have a reduced disposable income and, perhaps as importantly, there may be perceived uncertainty of incomes for those consumers not yet adversely affected. This uncertainty may manifest itself as a reluctance to experiment with a new expenditure.

In part the types of resistance referred to above reflect expectations that alter during an economic cycle and act to exacerbate any underlying swings in economic activity.

There is a further and more rational source of resistance, however, that accommodates the investment made in previous periods. According to conventional project or investment appraisal techniques, the availability of a new piece of plant, for example, should instigate a comparative analysis of the discounted net returns from the new and existing equipment. Subject to the new plant proving to be the more efficient use of funds a decision to invest would be made. In practice it is unlikely that behaviour follows these very calculated lines.

First there is the effect on secondhand prices. The appearance of new, highly efficient equipment that is fundamentally different from the equipment currently employed will depress secondhand prices: the impact on a balance sheet may be substantial and increase the requirement for additional funding that is not considered prudent by financiers.

Second, the appearance of new equipment that is economically efficient when delivered has no track record by implication: the reliability and back-up may jeopardize the value of the investment if these features do not match the distributors' or manufacturers' claims. With a completely new product based on new concepts, this uncertainty does exist and could be combined with the anticipation of reduced prices following the initial appearance and the elimination of teething troubles from subsequent models. Precisely the same rationale could inhibit the demand for durable consumer goods. There are also practical impediments that reflect the time and inconvenience of physically achieving the substitution of one piece of plant for another.

Finally, the course indicated by a comparative analysis of income streams from existing and new equipment may not be easily implemented in the event of the new equipment being demonstrably superior but requiring different skills and competences from its operators. This resistance would reflect any inflexibility in complementary factor markets and the delay in uptake of a demonstrably superior innovation would be governed by the least flexible factor market. For the catalytic entrepreneur, or the manager of a catalytic entrepreneurial event, it could be crucial to attempt to estimate when the resistance to the event's launch is lowest and so it can be supposed that events, first conceived at any point during an economic cycle, will have a tendency to appear as entrepreneurial events during the recovery and boom phases of a cycle. Furthermore, it might be supposed that it is the catalytic events developed within existing commercial organizations that are more governed by these strategic considerations. The cost of withholding an event that has already required substantial development funding would ordinarily be problematic for the individual or private entrepreneurial group.

A second trade-off appears for this non-corporate entrepreneur: in this case it is between the cost of overcoming heightened resistance in unfavourable economic conditions set against the costs of delaying the commercial appearance of the event. It is more likely that a catalytic event will be realized by a non-corporate entrepreneur so as to minimize costs rather than maximize the capitalized profit. As a consequence, there will not be a clustering of events from these entrepreneurs.

There is one further consideration for the non-corporate entrepreneur but exactly how the affect would influence the appearance of catalytic events is difficult to establish. In many cases it can be anticipated that a proposed entrepreneurial venture that is being promoted by a team or group of entrepreneurs will appear more credible and capable of faster realization to potential backers than one that has the commitment of only one individual. It has already been suggested that for the individual capitalist/entrepreneur a team could be recruited with the offer of salaries, but for the non-capitalist entrepreneur this option is not open. The opportunity cost of any entrepreneurial teams' labour will vary according to the buoyancy of particular sectors or the economy as a whole. In severely depressed conditions there may be potential team members with a low or zero opportunity cost: their commitment and support would be less expensive to recruit. If a complementary set of individuals could not be assembled from the unemployed, however, there may be a heightened resistance to sacrificing paid employment for a high-risk option when there is perceived to be little prospect of regaining employment in the event of the venture failing. A corollary would be the reduced reluctance to resign from salaried employment in buoyant conditions if the prospect of regaining alternative employment is high. In prosperous conditions the decision to pursue an entrepreneurial venture may be perceived to be reversible and the down-side risk perceived to be small, while in depressed conditions the decision may be perceived to be irreversible. Whether it can be supposed that entrepreneurial teams are established with greater or lesser ease at different points on an economic cycle will be determined by the employment status of the individuals concerned and their propensity to instigate or affiliate with catalytic entrepreneurial activity. These points are considered further in Chapter 9 where we examine the cyclical process in more detail.

RESISTANCE AND ENTREPRENEURIAL CREDIBILITY

The resistance which entrepreneurs, as a body, face will ebb and flow in line with the more general economic conditions; the resistance which an entrepreneur encounters will reflect the perceived credibility of the individual or individuals involved. If the credibility is incorrectly assessed by second and third parties then the resistance faced by an entrepreneur will not represent any useful, surrogate screening operation, but will have a wholly negative impact on the realization of the entrepreneurial event. In the case of an individual pursuing a catalytic event, which by definition, has no history, there is an onerous task of assembling a facade of credibility.

The credibility is required in the first instance to overcome the resistance of potential financiers and in the second instance to overcome the resistance of consumers. For the individual entrepreneur with substantial personal funds a team of individuals can be recruited who, when combined, have complementary skills and achievements that will appear credible to financiers.

Without the initial funds to cover the salaries of a team, alternative, less expensive, and probably more time-consuming approaches are required. These will more or less successfully achieve a similar result. The ease with which a non-funded approach will succeed will reflect the human capital or credibility of the prime mover and, in particular, the skills to convince and motivate the custodians of complementary human capital. Again these problems are greatly diminished, if not completely removed, for an entrepreneur within an existing organization. If the entrepreneur can generate the support and back-up of the employer, an entrepreneurial unit can be arranged more easily and the perceived credibility of that unit will be higher, everything else being equal. The single fact that an entrepreneur has employee status will generally enhance credibility; access to the organization's resources and network will give the venture a greater chance of success and a major potential problem of the entrepreneurial team being able to work together will be assumed to have been overcome.

In the early stages of gestation for an entrepreneurial event the perceived potential to be successful, however this is judged, is paramount. The criteria used by different assessors, whether they are potential backers or members of the team, will be different, but in principle the criteria will be more or less accurate indicators of the protagonist's human capital. The history of success and achievement, of the accumulation of tangible assets, will probably feature in this equation. Previous entrepreneurial failure may be seen by some assessors as useful and relevant experience, while by others it may be taken to expose the protagonist's inability to succeed with a new venture. Certainly a series of failures would not be viewed positively and it is in this situation that the suggestion of the entrepreneur bearing no risk can readily be seen to be untenable. It is the capitalist's role to provide finance but that finance is only available to the entrepreneur with a stock of human capital judged to be sufficient by the capitalist. The entrepreneur runs the risk of impairing that capital if a new venture does not succeed.

It is only surmised in passing that the breadth of knowledge and experience useful to the entrepreneur is unlikely to generate a CV that engenders credibility if only because of the apparent instability of the individual who has worked at different levels of responsibility, with different industries and in different regional or national economies. The corollary is that a scientist, for example, who has specialized in one discipline, focusing on one particular type of project and perhaps ideally placed to conceive of a highly sophisticated, technology-based entrepreneurial vision, will have had little or no opportunity to develop the wider skills necessary to develop a complementary team that has the credibility to generate funds to progress the event's gestation.

A major constraint to realized entrepreneurship of the catalytic category could be expected to emanate from the inability to organize a complementary set of individuals who are prepared to risk human capital on the one hand and either personal finances or future income on the other. In the light of the foregoing it almost becomes unrealistic to expect there to be entrepreneurial activity of the catalytic type pursued by entrepreneurs who are not either employed by an organization which can accommodate entrepreneurship or who are personally the holders of very substantial funds.

THE ALLOCATING ENTREPRENEUR

This entrepreneur pursues an event that presents a genuinely new combination of resources but the feature that distinguishes the allocating event is that the origin of the combination can be traced to a previous commercial application. Examples of the allocating event would include the introduction of an adapted product, process or service to an industrial sector or region that had hitherto failed to appreciate the benefit of a particular principle or component that was applied in another industry. Allocating activity would include refining a particular output and presenting it to a market established perhaps by other allocating entrepreneurs or perhaps a market established by catalytic entrepreneurs. Allocating activity would include satisfying a new demand that results from a successful catalytic event or one that has emerged from the changing of tastes and preferences of consumers.

Allocating entrepreneurs are most adept at exploiting the possibility for arbitrage and although this activity could be perceived as the work of catalytic entrepreneurs within a micro- or industry-specific context, the underlying components and principles of the event could be observed, commercially applied, elsewhere within the economy. The ingenuity and imagination of the allocating entrepreneur is not belittled but the original creativity of the catalytic entrepreneur is missing and indeed unnecessary.

The allocating entrepreneur has to undertake similar operations to those undertaken by the catalytic entrepreneur. The resistance, however, encountered by this entrepreneur will ordinarily be less than that faced by the catalytic entrepreneur for the principal reason that the proposed combination of resources has a precedent which can be held to demonstrate that a previous application has been successful. Even where an application had achieved only dubious viability it can be an easier task to demonstrate that the identified shortcomings have been avoided rather than introduce a completely new concept. Those individuals whose approval is required before the event can be presented to market; bankers and private investors, for example, can at least more readily grasp the idea; they will be less likely to react negatively on the basis of a desire to conceal ignorance or invest time in understanding a proposal that might still be judged unviable when the understanding has been achieved. Similarly, consumer resistance would ordinarily be reduced.

An alternative way of viewing this resistance would be as the reduced cost of educating second and third parties. Education would still be required but the form of education could shift towards advertising and promotion. Successful allocating events can be the inspiration for other allocating activity where the product, service or process is tailored to the requirements of a potential market not previously satisfied. With each application the combination of resources can be refined and there can be a long and steady history of adaptations and improvements so that the current output bears little resemblance to its antecedent. Allocating entrepreneurs in this way can promote gradualistic change and movement towards a production possibility frontier but nothing so fundamental that implications of any one event disjoint the circular flow. Within established commercial organizations that supply a fashion-orientated and competitive market, the process of product life-cycles and the allocating event is familiar to the extent that the allocating activity can almost be routinized. In such situations the entrepreneur will probably be a specialist team with complementary skills, access to supportive networks and an intimate familiarity with many of the markets that provide the goods and services necessary for the efficient development of an allocating event. As with catalytic activity, the precise occurrence of the allocating vision can not be specified but the strategic considerations regarding the rate of development, and particularly the launch, will not be a matter of chance. The event managed by corporate entrepreneurs will be realized when the prospect for success is greatest or when the commercial life of existing products or processes is expected to be terminating.

Allocating activity represents proactivity. The activity can be prompted or encouraged by the anticipated behaviour of customers or competitors and in that sense it is reactive, but, for allocating activity defined here, something new is created—some product or process becomes available that was not available before. The output represents a compatible element in a wider progression that needs little explaining in retrospect. Allocating activity is gradualistic or evolutionary and can be contrasted so plainly with a potent catalytic event. This characteristic in itself suggests that the difficulties encountered by the purveyors of the event, although similar in nature, will differ in magnitude.

Despite the relative ease of orchestrating the allocating event suggested above, it is crucial to acknowledge that opportunities arise either because of changing tastes and preferences, i.e. economic pressures, or because of endogenous and exogenous shocks. In the absence of these disturbances to the economic system the potential for allocating activity will become increasingly restricted. The notion of diminishing marginal returns can be employed to convey the idea of increasing difficulty encountered by allocating entrepreneurs to create new opportunities in a world where nothing is changing. Ultimately there will come a point when it is no longer economic for existing organizations to retain allocating entrepreneurs and those events occurring will be of increasingly insignificant impact, perpetrated by the private individual or groups of individuals.

The constraints restricting allocating entrepreneurship will be substantially similar in character, although reduced in scale, to those faced by catalytic entrepreneurs. The difference between catalytic and allocating entrepreneurs, however, is that the potential for allocating activity is related to shocks or pressures in the economic system whereas potential catalytic activity is completely independent of other types of entrepreneurial activity. It is thus conceivable for there to be a swarming of entrepreneurs as Schumpeter described but the swarming does not indicate a breakdown of the resistance discussed earlier; rather it indicates the realization of a catalytic event that has created potential for substantial allocating activity. The observations concerning the timing of realized events in relation to macroeconomic conditions hold here as before. For the reasons discussed earlier, it can be expected that allocating events pursued by corporate entrepreneurs will tend to appear when economic conditions are judged to be favourable, whereas allocating events pursued by non-corporate entrepreneurs may appear to minimize pre-sales expenditure.

THE REFINING ENTREPRENEUR

This is perhaps the least glamorous and least conspicuous entrepreneur who pursues the prospect of profit by introducing innovations that improve the resource-use efficiency of existing operations without affecting the potential of those operations. The combination of resources may be altered through the introduction of attitudes, practices, and equipment that are not conventional within the industry. Successful innovations of this type do not produce new goods or services that directly generate additional income, but are for internal use with a view to reducing the costs or increasing output of familiar operations or products.

In a competitive market that is not being driven forward by the appearance of competitors exploiting catalytic and allocating events, the only prospect of achieving improved performance is through intra-business efficiency. A firm's competitive advantage may rely exclusively on internal efficiency resulting from entrepreneurial activity: there are clear reasons why these innovations will not be publicized. The requirement for entrepreneurship within existing organizations becomes more pronounced as the profit from an initiating catalytic or allocating development is eroded. In organizations, where temporary monopoly profit is still available, there is the luxury of being able to accommodate more mundane, operational inefficiency without jeopardizing the organization's existence. New or amended markets and expenditure patterns, brought about by catalytic and allocating activity, will have negative implications for some firms that have traditionally held a position in the circular flow. The adversely affected firms can react by pursuing refining activity. Depending upon the amount of inefficiency originally existing, the refining activity may be successful in protracting the traditional operation for a greater or shorter period. The scope for activity within existing operations is confined by the definitions used here and it can be supposed that diminishing marginal returns will be detected in relation to increasing expenditure on refining entrepreneurial effort. Whereas the catalytic and allocating events managed by existing organizations will appear according to strategic considerations, the appearance of refining events within existing organizations will tend to reflect more tactical considerations. If corporate catalytic and allocating activity can be released in periods of economic buoyancy, during recovery and boom phases of a cycle, and there are time-lags before the adverse effects are perceived by the traditional businesses, then the pressure for refining activity could be expected to increase as the cycle turned from boom to recessionary phases.

The resistance encountered by refining entrepreneurs will differ from that faced by catalytic and allocating entrepreneurs. The markets in which refining entrepreneurs operate are established and familiar: it is possible for these entrepreneurs to have completely relevant track records. The resistance that is faced will be more likely to emanate from within the organization or from within the industry. For the non-corporate entrepreneur establishing a new business, the refining event would be the easiest to achieve: the potential for growth and development, however, may be constrained without subsequent entrepreneurial activity. The credibility gap for the refining entrepreneur is more easily overcome and the financial implications of this could be significant, first in terms of the sums required and secondly in terms of the number of sources of funds available. The resistance faced by the refining entrepreneur occurs when existing traders within the particular market react negatively or hostilely to a new entrant. The time taken to establish a position within existing markets could be a significant constraint on the development and expansion of a new business pursuing the profits of a refining event.

One outcome of refining activity could be the release of surplus resources. In particular, labour and plant might be shed to accommodate new practices and declining or squeezed markets. The appearance of these resources, everything else being held equal, would depress their prices and further facilitate the emergence of non-corporate entrepreneurs. In certain cases, the employee within a traditional industry may take the depressed factor prices as the trigger to resign and pursue a refining vision that had been gently nurtured for a number of years and is now made possible by the relatively cheap factor inputs which are required.

THE OMEGA ENTREPRENEUR

The omega entrepreneur is a specific subgroup of the refining entrepreneur. The conditions which stimulate the appearance of an omega entrepreneur are very similar to those referred to in the preceding paragraph: depressed conditions within a specific industrial sector or more generally, can stimulate a planned liquidation of redundant plant or promote compulsory liquidations where those assets are disposed of with little attention to the prices offered. The low prices may trigger the resignation of individuals who plan to exploit some event, but occurring simultaneously will be the release of labour. The labour and plant released from a declining industrial sector will be complementary and as the opportunity cost of the plant is low so the opportunity cost of a part of the labour will be low: from an economic point of view, it may be zero. Certainly where the mobility of labour is restricted and the investment in human capital can not easily be supplemented, there could be an attraction for this labour and plant to recombine as a new small business. Often there can be no perceived constraints to this kind of entrepreneurial activity. The requirement for finance can be minimal and working for low or negative incomes in the short term might be considered preferable to being unemployed.

Whereas catalytic, allocating, and refining entrepreneurial activity can be observed at any phase of an economic cycle, with the corporate catalytic and allocating activity exhibiting a propensity to appear in recovery/boom conditions and refining activity concentrating in boom/recession conditions, omega activity is restricted to conditions characterized by contracting employment prospects. Those omega entrepreneurs appearing will exclusively comprise private individuals or groups: there will not be the corporate omega entrepreneurs and the activity will not be arranged to fulfil wider strategic or tactical considerations. The entrepreneurial event will be arranged to minimize costs and gestation time. This activity, although reflecting lack of opportunity, is genuinely entrepreneurial in so far as the combination of resources is without precedent because the cost conditions are novel. An alternative reaction, but one that is clearly differentiated, would be for the redundant labour to combine with other factors to replicate an existing small business type. Omega entrepreneurship is unlikely to encounter resistance in forms similar to that experienced by the other categories of entrepreneurs. The principal constraint will be restricted demand reflecting the conditions of a declining industry.

SUMMARY

The factor market for entrepreneurship is not an overt or easily scrutinized market. Indeed there is no market in a conventional sense; nevertheless, there are economic conditions when the opportunities for entrepreneurship are greater and the speed with which opportunities are realized will be a determinant of economic change. From a policy point of view the demand for entrepreneurship, and more particularly, specific types of entrepreneurship, will vary. Similarly, there are economic conditions that induce entrepreneurial activity and affect the apparent supply. There is no straightforward, co-ordinating mechanism between supply and demand, however, and therefore a mismatch can be anticipated from a macro perspective.

The acceptance of entrepreneurship being a largely spontaneous activity is not helpful in so far as the appearance of an entrepreneurial event is the termination of a gestation period which can be managed, brought forward and held back, according to the judgement of the entrepreneur. Corporate entrepreneurs will be more subject to strategic and tactical considerations and their activity can be expected to exacerbate fluctuations in the level of economic activity. Private entrepreneurial activity will be realized in a less predictable manner. However there is still the potential for peaks of activity to occur.

If the notion of diminishing marginal returns is relevant to the volume of allocating and refining entrepreneurial activity, then the random appearance of a potent catalytic event, an endogenous shock to the economic system, will increase the unexploited stock of potential allocating events and, everything else being equal, increase the appearance of allocating entrepreneurs. The realized catalytic and allocating entrepreneurial events combined, by altering previous patterns of expenditure, will have negative implications for traditional firms and stimulate the reaction of refining activity elsewhere in the economy.

Entrepreneurs will encounter resistance because of their challenge to the status quo and the resistance faced by the catalytic entrepreneurs in particular will reflect the novelty of the innovation and the perceived credibility of the entrepreneur by second and third parties. The distinction between capitalists and entrepreneurs is accepted but this distinction can not be used to suggest that the entrepreneur bears no risk. The perceived human capital/credibility is put at risk by the entrepreneur and it is the entrepreneur's investment of this capital which generates the entrepreneurial profit.

A further distinction within a discussion of the supply of entrepreneurship revolves around the final status of the apparent entrepreneurial activity. Whereas a perceived requirement for entrepreneurs implicitly refers to successful or viable entrepreneurship, there is a significant chance that an entrepreneurial event is aborted or is, more or less, unsuccessful from a financial point of view. Attempts to increase the supply of entrepreneurship are not successful if they promote the appearance of entrepreneurial events that are not viable. A reduction in the volume of entrepreneurial activity accompanied by a higher success rate would be more efficient and simultaneously reduce the resistance which confronts catalytic and allocating entrepreneurs.

The resistance faced by entrepreneurs is more apparent when it is presented by second and third parties, but resistance could emanate from the potential entrepreneur if there were known to be gaps in personal experience and knowledge of the instigator. In particular, a core of commercial training would complement any subsequent business experience, facilitate an early assessment of a potential entrepreneurial venture, crucially supplement the human capital of the entrepreneur, and engender confidence and familiarity with the principles of business. Together these outcomes would reduce internal and external resistance to entrepreneurial activity. Furthermore, it emerges from the arguments that a failure to differentiate between the types of entrepreneurs could promote entrepreneurial activity that is inefficient in so far as diminishing marginal returns have set in for additional allocating and refining entrepreneurial activity and that the cost and risk of failure have risen to unacceptable levels. A limited, but focused, attention on catalytic entrepreneurship could be more efficient in so far as it is from these entrepreneurs that the potential for allocating entrepreneurs emerges and it is from catalytic and allocating entrepreneurs combined that the stimuli for refining entrepreneurs is generated.

Factors that restrict the imagination/knowledge of individuals will constrain entrepreneurship. Considerations that reduce the flexibility of factor markets, in particular the finance and labour markets, will constrain entrepreneurship.

Factors that increase the uncertainty faced by entrepreneurs will restrict entrepreneurship.

Factors that reduce the effective entrepreneurial profit flowing to entrepreneurs will reduce entrepreneurship.

These sources of constraint impinge more or less directly on social and political systems rather than on the economic system *per se*. The culture of society will determine the flows of knowledge and the freedom for imagination: legislation and restrictive practices will account for much inflexibility in factor markets. Political and social stability will reduce the uncertainty faced by entrepreneurs, and the fiscal arrangements and laws relating to royalties, patents, and the allocation of legal costs will affect the size and duration of temporary monopolistic profits.

Many of these issues are outside the scope of the present discussion and only the factor markets are considered further. The following chapter discusses the factor market for finance.

CHAPTER
SIX

THE FACTOR MARKET FOR FINANCE

INTRODUCTION

The factor market for finance is crucially important to the entrepreneur. The more readily finance can be obtained, the more easily other difficulties and constraints can be overcome. If the factor market for finance does not function efficiently and the flow of funds to entrepreneurial activity is restricted, then if everything else is held equal, there will be reduced activity. There is a trade-off between human capital within an entrepreneurial team and the quantity of finance that is necessary to pursue an entrepreneurial event. The larger the team and the broader the skills and expertise contained, the lower the incurred fees for necessary input and, simultaneously, other factor markets can be used more proficiently and cost-effectively.

The amount and type of finance required to develop and exploit an entrepreneurial event can vary greatly. The amount of finance will be determined by the associated development costs, particular set-up costs and the more familiar costs of fixed assets and working capital. There are decisions to be made that influence the amount of funding required by directly affecting the risk accepted by the entrepreneur. A clear illustration would be the trade-off between the market intelligence available and expenditure on market research: similarly there is a relationship between marketing expenditure and expected sales. Entrepreneurs with different attitudes to risk aversion could have substantially different financial requirements for the same project. It is important to recognize, however, that for a given level of risk aversion, the amount of finance required for a given project will be determined by the costs established in the markets confronted. Imperfections which increase the costs incurred by the entrepreneur in any of the markets faced will act to reduce the likelihood of an entrepreneurial venture being profitable and increase the amount of finance required.

The factor market for finance is central to the entrepreneurs' activities: it is unique in so far as some finance is usually necessary to access the market over and above any transaction costs. The factor market for finance is complex, fulfilling different functions and demanding different protocols: specialized experience and knowledge is often necessary to use the markets efficiently.

In the case of an entrepreneur operating within a profitable organization, the problems of generating finance will ordinarily be reduced subject to the scale of the proposed venture in relation to the status of the company and the board's full commitment. For the entrepreneur outside an employing organization, who personally holds sufficient assets and can simultaneously act as capitalist/investor, there will clearly be no difficulty generating funds. Here however, it is the private entrepreneur who does not have the personal wealth to finance the venture—or the support of an existing business—who will be focused upon, for it is in this case that constraints can be most clearly illustrated. The considerations discussed will apply more or less severely to other types of entrepreneur.

It is important to recognize that there are phases or milestones during the gestation period of an entrepreneurial event. Ordinarily, the requirement for finance to cover fixed assets and trading expenses will be associated with one of the final phases. The gestation period for an entrepreneurial event is determined in part by the nature and implications of the project and in part by the amount of finance that is available. The amount of finance required varies substantially between one venture and another and between one entrepreneur and another, but also the expected pattern, duration, and magnitude of returns varies. One consequence of this heterogeneity of financial requirements is that the factor market for finance comprises factor markets for categories of finance. Applications for funds have to be matched to the activities of the investor and misdirected applications are unlikely to be successful.

Reflecting the various factor markets for finance and the heterogeneity of financial requirements, our discussion will be approached according to the generic types of funding rather than according to the classification of entrepreneurs and entrepreneurial events used in preceding chapters. Generally, however, it can be assumed that the risk associated with the categories of entrepreneurial event isolated will be greatest for the catalytic event and least for the refining event. In the case of the catalytic event there is some element of the product, process, service, or system that is completely new and unknown by definition. As a consequence there is uncertainty associated with the development being realized and viable in practice. Combined with this is the prospect of positive income streams not occurring in the short term due to unforeseeable obstacles in the development and marketing strategies and inevitable teething problems. To accommodate the risk of the development being unsuccessful and the timing of returns being unpredictable, the catalytic event is most appropriately financed with funds that participate in the risk and reward of the investment.

For the refining event the innovation focuses upon increased efficiency, or more appropriately the removal of inefficiency, within a proposed operation that has close parallels already operating in a commercial environment. With the replication of existing operations a base level of return can be estimated for additional investment. The refining event, then, is concerned with the 'less risky' issue of justifying returns above this base level which itself represents a floor to the downside risk. These considerations imply that the prominence of participating funds can be reduced and substituted for by non-participating loans. The allocating event would fall somewhere between the catalytic event and the refining event. As such it would be anticipated that prudent combinations of finance would reflect this intermediate position.

Additionally, it can be assumed that the pre-trading, research, and development expenses of the catalytic event will exceed those associated with refining events, although this is not necessarily the case. The scale of funding for the complete implementation of any particular category of entrepreneurial event, however, can not be usefully generalized.

GENERIC FUNDING INSTRUMENTS

The range and scope of financial instruments is large and continually evolving. Nevertheless, all instruments fit more or less neatly into a continuum that is confined by pure-risk, or participating, capital at one extreme and risk-free, or non-participating, capital at the other. For the provider of funds, pure-risk capital is abbreviated to equity and restricted to ordinary-share capital: risk-free capital is fully secured debt capital. In the simple classical model an introductory economic treatment takes the price of debt to be the rate of interest. If the demand for, or supply of, loanable funds alters, the rate of interest moves to restore a market clearing balance. Similarly, company shares can be put to the market: the price realized reflects an anticipated return adjusted for risk that at the margin, makes the capitalist/investor indifferent to investments in shares or loans. The oversimplification of such treatments conceals the idiosyncrasies of the markets and the imperfections generated at a micro and macro level that can substantially distort the mechanism of a competitive ideal.

EQUITY FINANCE

Equity is pure-risk capital and represents the amount of money that the owners of a business entity are liable to lose in the event of the venture being unsuccessful. Equity that is provided by the entrepreneur or by other executive personnel is referred to as internal equity. Alternatively, equity can be provided by third parties who buy a shareholding that provides them with a saleable right to a specific portion of any future dividends. Equity bought by third parties is referred to as external equity. Holders of the ordinary shares of a company have no recourse in the event of complete failure.

Equity finance is particularly important in the case of entrepreneurial activity because of the associated risk that the venture will fail. The relevance of equity is sometimes disguised in more modest ventures and in unincorporated businesses in particular. The fact that the entrepreneur has generated the financial equity by a fully secured personal loan does not matter: the original source of the funds invested in equity is irrelevant; rather it is relevant that the personally secured loan represents the extent of the liability that the entrepreneur is obliged to discharge and has, by virtue of the security, demonstrated that it can be fully discharged in the case of default.

In new private limited companies the registered holding of ordinary shares can be very small, but in practice this will often be supplemented by loans to the business that are personally guaranteed by the directors, or by a form of directors' loan which has special and binding conditions applying to the withdrawal of funds from the business. Although these funds are not recorded as shares in a balance sheet they represent effective equity or quasi equity. In practice, it is irrelevant where the individuals generate the funds to buy the equity or quasi equity of a business; what is relevant is the inescapability of effective equity for any type of legitimate entrepreneurial venture. The value of equity within an entrepreneurial venture will have implications for the value of debt that can be generated by the business and is distinct from the value of debt that can be generated by the individual owners of the business.

The sum of internally generated equity may reflect the wealth of the participating individuals and their commitment to the entrepreneurial activity as often as it represents a prudent minimum required to develop the entrepreneurial venture. For very practical and mundane reasons there are finite limits to the equity that can be generated internally. For anything other than modest ventures the amount of equity required is likely to exceed that available internally. The entrepreneur is then obliged to consider external investors if the venture is to proceed.

The market for shares in private limited companies bears little resemblance to the perfectly competitive ideal. Any agreement that is struck represents the outcome of negotiation, often with significant time delays, substantial administrative and preparation costs and the balance of power often resting with the investor. It is important to recognize that there is not an established market in the shares of private limited companies and that there is still less of a market for the shares of those that have not yet traded and have no track record. Furthermore, the organizations and individuals prepared to buy these shares have only short track records themselves and typically limited experience in assembling their portfolios. Similarly, entrepreneurs requiring external equity are often unfamiliar with the investors, with their protocol and criteria and often the implications of an external equity investment. In part it is for these reasons that there is a reluctance among entrepreneurs to seek the participation of external investors and venture capitalists in particular.

It is also worth noting that there can be a reluctance on the part of entrepreneurs to seek external participation because of the very principle of this type of funding. The entrepreneur can be protective of the vision and resent third parties being involved, because they would take a portion of the embryonic business, have an influence over the way the affair is managed, and possibly—most difficult to reconcile of all—have a claim on a percentage of the profits generated by the vision, skill, toil, and endeavour of the entrepreneur. Half a loaf is better than none, but this type of rationale is irrelevant to some emotive entrepreneurs. It is the prerogative of the entrepreneur to avoid external equity and to pursue the event, possibly undercapitalized and with greatly increased odds of failure. This raises the problem of successful and unsuccessful entrepreneurship: the quality of the vision and the potential of the event may be high, but the actual or perceived conditions tied to external equity may halt the potential event's development or promote undercapitalized ventures that have high failure rates.

From the investors' point of view this stance may seem completely incomprehensible. The funds at their disposal have alternative uses and the risk of failure is viewed more objectively.

INVESTOR/SUPPLIER PREFERENCES

For those individuals or organizations prepared to buy the shares in private limited companies, the main considerations refer to the anticipated return. The return would ordinarily take the form of a capital gain upon the disposal of the shares, rather than an income stream generated on the share holding. In the United Kingdom this preference represents the effective marginal rates of tax on capital gains and income. Should the relative rates of tax alter, this preference will change. Again, because of the limited market for the shares in private limited companies, it can be difficult for external investors to find a willing buyer when they wish to liquidate their shareholding. If there is no foreseeable exit route for the external equity investor, the investment is unlikely to be made. If fiscal changes reversed the current preference for capital gains over income, a major constraint on external investment would be removed.

Investment in an entrepreneurial venture is unlikely to yield a return for a number of years: the uncertainty associated with the investment is high as is its illiquidity. Furthermore, the net return to the investor has to accommodate evaluation and monitoring costs, as well as the probability that some investments will fail and that investment in some proposals investigated will not be made. In part, to contain evaluation and monitoring costs, investors often restrict the entrepreneurial proposals they will consider to specific industrial sectors and geographical locations. As it is expensive for the entrepreneur to assemble and present the information required by investors, so it is expensive for the investor to evaluate the realism and integrity of the information. Once the investor's funds have been committed, monitoring is required to oversee the stewardship of the funds. This can be seen by entrepreneurs as an unnecessary and unwelcome facet of external equity.

The holding of ordinary shares by the external investors will provide them with some corporate power to determine the way the business is run. The ordinary shares and associated voting rights will reflect the outcome of negotiation between the investor and the investee but from the investor's point of view, the percentage of shares sought will reflect the anticipated performance of the business. In particular the capitalized value of the business at the end of the preferred time horizon will represent 100 per cent of the ordinary shares and provide the denominator for the required financial return of the investor. The investor's required return divided by the anticipated value of the business will set the minimum shareholding sought. In practice this figure is often manipulated by combining debt and equity packages so that the shareholding taken is between 20 per cent and 30 per cent, while the required return on that holding is equivalent to between 25 per cent and 35 per cent compound per year. The upshot of this is that the growth rate of a business must be very high over a period where entrepreneurial skills and insight must be substituted by effective management skills.

The human capital embodied within the entrepreneurial team is crucially important to the success of the venture and therefore to the potential investor. Accurate assessments of this kind are impossible to achieve, however, and the final investment decision does not so much reflect a ranking of prospective financial returns within a few points of each other, but rather, subjective opinions and biases about the strengths and weaknesses of the entrepreneurial team.

Finally it must be recognized explicitly that the evaluation, administration, negotiation, and monitoring costs of the investor do not vary in strict proportion to the sum of finance being invested. These costs are more usefully thought of as fixed costs and as such imply minimum investments below which the effective costs of an investment are prohibitive. In practice this minimum currently lies around £150 000. Increased efficiency among investors, in particular, the ability to evaluate proposals accurately and reduce the proportion of failures within their portfolios, would, everything else being held equal, reduce the effective minimum investment that was economic. The equity gap, that is the absence of equity finance in parcels below the economic minimum of the specialized organizations, is often cited as a constraint restricting entrepreneurial activity in new and small firms. For individuals with surplus funds that they would be willing to invest as a third party in an entrepreneurial event, there is an opportunity to avoid some of the overhead costs incurred by the professional investors. The evaluation and monitoring costs of the individual investor in particular can be lower but in practice very little funding flows directly from third-party individuals to entrepreneurs. In part this reflects the presumed and actual lack of expertise by the individual investors who can, as an alternative, subscribe to an investment fund with professional managers and expertise; in part, it reflects a lack of effective channels for the private investor and entrepreneur to make contact and, in part, it reflects a general lack of familiarity and activity in these types of investments. It is interesting to note that the equity gap was first investigated in the United Kingdom in the late 1920s and its appearance was accredited to the demise of a mythical Aunt Agatha. Aunt Agatha represented a private investor in new and small businesses whose investment overhead costs were substantially reduced by a particular closeness to the entrepreneur. Although efforts have been made in UK policy to close the equity gap, provision has never been made to encourage the re-emergence of Aunt Agatha-type investors. Tax concessions to individual equity investors in the United Kingdom, for example, explicitly exclude investments by linearly related parties.

ENTREPRENEURS' PREFERENCES

From the discussion of equity there can be isolated a number of circumstances under which a potentially successful entrepreneurial event may never be realized or may be attempted with a substantially reduced chance of success.

If the entrepreneur, be it an individual or group, can not generate sufficient equity from internal sources, and opposes external equity in principle, then the venture is either halted or pursued under-capitalized with a greater risk of failure. At first sight there is little to address this problem although creativity with regard to novel personal debt instruments may have a significant impact. This is explored in more detail in Part Three.

If external equity investors are inept at identifying potentially successful entrepreneurs, the failure rates of their investments will be higher, as will their monitoring and administrative costs. The upshot of this would be to increase the target return on investments and to raise the effective minimum equity investment. Both outcomes would reduce the number of qualifying proposals. As it is, there would be a great problem to establish the number of entrepreneurial events delayed or lost because the external equity requirement or the projected return is less than the economic minimum dictated by the current efficiency of investors. Whatever the range of the effective equity gap, the range of the actual funding gap for entrepreneurial ventures will be larger by virtue of possible financial gearing: this is considered in more detail in the section on debt funding.

From the entrepreneur's point of view, external equity participation is generally considered only when there is limited and insufficient equity available from internal sources. Furthermore, an approach to an external investor probably follows several unsuccessful attempts to generate debt. Although it is not always the case, an approach to generate equity from commercial investors is often perceived as the source of last resort. One explanation of this perception is the cost and rigmarole of even securing an opportunity to present a case to an investor. For the entrepreneur with inadequate finance to pursue a vision there is an understandable reluctance to invest time and money in preparations and presentations that at best will tie an unwanted third party into the business and, at worst, may rob the venture of the prospect of even continuing, albeit underfunded. Policy at a local and national level has been devised that could be argued to reduce the effective cost of approaching equity investors: such schemes provide grants towards consultancy, research, and presentation expenses. In practice these schemes have had a substantially reduced impact because of the capitalization of grants into the pricing structures of the intermediaries and because of the ineffective evaluation of the competences of the intermediaries themselves.

The factors which lead to the approach and presentation costs are particularly illuminating in so far as they represent a characteristic of the market for the external equity which could have a major impact on apparent entrepreneurial activity and the number of realized entrepreneurial events. The obligation of an entrepreneur soliciting external equity is to provide a case that addresses fundamental issues regarding the quantity of finance required, how the funds are to be allocated, and the anticipated level of profit. For the entrepreneur's case to be successful it must be convincing and supported by the best data available. The crucial feature of this procedure is that perfect data are unavailable, that the future is always unknown and that the data can be hugely expensive to obtain, analyse, and professionally present. It is a matter of judgement as to whether attempts to gather and process additional information are worthwhile. Any judgement made will reflect an attitude to risk. If the potential investor's attitude to risk is different from that of the entrepreneur then the entrepreneur and potential investor will be convinced by different amounts of data.

In view of the qualities required by an entrepreneur, it might be supposed that the entrepreneur will invest finance in the project where the external investor would not. In cases where external equity is required for an entrepreneurial event to be pursued, it is the investor's assessment of risk and not the entrepreneur's that is paramount. Constraints upon entrepreneurial activity, therefore, can appear when the investor is relatively risk-averse or the costs of assembling the data are greater than the entrepreneur can personally finance. Finally it must be recognized that potential investors themselves will perceive a similar risk differently and require different packages of information before investing in a particular project. The precise requirements of any one potential investor are unlikely to be known by the entrepreneur beforehand: an additional element of risk is introduced for the entrepreneur in these circumstances and an extra potential for personal funds created.

From the foregoing it is unequivocally the case that the entrepreneur is generally a capitalist to some degree, even if this capital is relatively minor in relation to the total external funds ultimately employed. The entrepreneur is, therefore, exposed to financial risk in the orthodox sense, in addition to bearing the risk associated with the investment of human capital discussed in the previous chapter.

DEBT FINANCE

Secured debt or loan finance in a pure form carries no risk for the lender. The loan represents a preference on the part of the lender for a guaranteed income stream over a given term while the borrower has a preference for a capital sum and is prepared to set aside future income to repay the capital and interest according to a mutually agreed schedule. The loan is risk-free for the lender when collateral against the loan has a net realizable value at least as great as the original loan. In practice many loans do carry some risk and premiums will be charged to accommodate the perceived risk of default.

It is necessary to differentiate clearly between debt generated by a private individual and debt generated by a business. Confusion is easily introduced if this distinction is not recognized. In the case of entrepreneurial activity pursued by an entrepreneur ouside an existing business, it can be difficult to disentangle the nature of any debt generated. Reference has already been made to the phases in the gestation period of an entrepreneurial event. That gestation is only successfully completed when the original vision has been enacted and has resulted in a profit-generating operation. The beginning of the gestation period is characterized in the case we are exploring by the absence of a business. At some point during the gestation period the entrepreneur ceases to be an individual or group of individuals and becomes a business. The legal status of the business can vary, but whatever the status, there is usually a precise date when the activities of the entrepreneur become a business, from legal and fiscal perspectives. From an economic perspective, however, no such precise date exists. The entrepreneur has the germ of a vision as an individual and nurtures that vision to a greater or lesser extent before attempting to develop it. The early phases of development may proceed with no financial outlay on the part of the entrepreneur. There will be investment of time but this may not be substantial. There may be small 'out of pocket' expenses that in the early stages can not be distinguished as either business expenses or personal expenses.

Depending upon the strategy of the entrepreneur, more significant expenses will be incurred sooner or later in the development process. These expenses can be met either from liquidity held by the entrepreneur or by liquidity generated from some form of loan. If the entrepreneur raises a loan, guarantees or security will be required. Whether or not the entrepreneur chooses to declare the activity as a business is only relevant from a fiscal point of view but not relevant from a lender's point of view. The 'business' has no security in these embryonic stages of development and has no income of its own to provide a guarantee. Clearly if the entrepreneur has no assets, liquid or otherwise, these pre-business expenses cannot be incurred.

As the stage of development progresses the accumulated pre-business expenses will increase and the likelihood of a requirement for personal loans becomes greater. At the point where further pre-business loans are not available, to the individual or individuals concerned, either the entrepreneurial event is aborted, or external equity is required. Imperfections in the finance market for personal debt can be significant in terms of restricted access to liquidity for investment in equity. The conditions under which such restrictions appear are similar to those which would restrict the generation of corporate debt and are addressed later in this section. In view of the discussion of the costs associated with raising external equity, the probability of generating external equity with no personal assets is ignored. Informal loans and gifts may be available from family and friends but we are not in a position to discuss the implications of these, and we assume that the potential for generating informal loans has ended when the entrepreneur cannot generate further personal funds. The entrepreneurial event could be resurrected after a period of more orthodox paid employment, or after restructuring the entrepreneurial team to include an individual with adequate wealth to develop the event further—possibly to the point of securing additional external equity and beyond.

Subject to satisfactory development, and either internal or external equity, there can begin the more overt 'set up' phase of the gestation. Included in this phase could be the purchase or lease of premises, plant and machinery acquisitions, promotional literature and the purchase of stock, installation of services, incorporation fees, etc. But also included would be specific customer research that could only be undertaken when the venture is in a position to offer a product or service for sale. It would not be until the business itself owned assets, however, that the business could generate debt and it is from this point of development that our discussion continues.

A competitive market for debt in a neo-classical sense would allocate funds according to the borrower's willingness to pay and the borrower's ability to secure the debt. Since the new business is still not able to generate an income, the valuation of the security concerned can become critical. Much of the firm's financial equity on day one will be used to cover expenditure on items and costs that have no security value by virtue of the non-saleable quality of the purchases. It is only that expenditure on easily liquidated assets that can be used to generate debt. Furthermore, the extent to which original equity can be used to generate debt will be reduced by a liquidator's fraction or carcass evaluation of the saleable assets. The severity of the valuation procedure will alter according to the particular assets involved. For unusual pieces of machinery, manufactured to fulfil a particular role, for example, the discount price could be as low as its scrap value. This type of valuation reflects the lender's aversion to holding an *ad hoc* collection of assets until such time as a willing buyer is found. Clearly the more unusual the combination of resources being assembled by the entrepreneur, the greater the likelihood that willing buyers will only be found with difficulty, and the more problematic it is for the entrepreneur to generate useful quantities of debt. The more conventional and saleable the assets the more debt could be generated. This understandable requirement of debt providers would dis-advantage the more entrepreneurial activity to a greater extent than it would orthodox and traditional new businesses.

It is only after a new business has been successfully trading for a period that assets will be valued on a going-concern basis. To develop this track record, finance is required to cover the working-capital component of the new business and typically working capital has little or no intrinsic collateral value. Particular raw materials may be exceptional, precious metals would be a prime example; similarly blue-chip debtors may be taken as security and easily sold finished goods may be valued but work in progress is typically ascribed zero collateral value and most debtors and stocks are financed from equity which involves a reduction in a business's ability to generate debt.

Debt can be provided by the suppliers of working capital and fixed assets in the form of trade credit or HP/leasing arrangements but it is important to note that these trade suppliers of debt may also be reluctant to negotiate with an entrepreneurial venture that has no track record of profitable business. Furthermore, the more unique the requirements of the entrepreneurial venture the more problematic the generation of trade debt becomes. In the case of plant and machinery, an entrepreneurial venture may require the equipment to be built on a bespoke basis for which the prospect of leasing is unavailable and for which interim payments are necessary before the equipment is available. There are negative cash flow implications when the entrepreneurial venture has such requirements in addition to the more severe collateral valuations.

LENDER/SUPPLIER PREFERENCES

Lenders ideally prefer to lend in circumstances where the risk of default is zero, where the interest charged is as high as possible, and where transactions and administration costs are minimized.

The collateral or security sought by a lender has already been discussed: where collateral values are set at unnecessarily low levels the borrower may experience a constraint upon the ability to generate debt. Competition among lenders would ensure that interest charged in a perfect world equated supply with demand. If the number of lenders is smaller than that necessary to guarantee effective competition or there are a number of lenders with some degree of market power, there is scope for strategies of joint profit maximization in the absence of effective regulation. In the extreme position of there being only one lender, monopoly profit becomes available. Any uncorrected imperfections in the market from a supply side will restrict the supply of debt and, everything else being equal, allow larger profits to accrue to lenders at the expense of entrepreneurial activity. Transaction and administration costs per unit of currency lent decline as the value of the debt increases. Even for ambitious entrepreneurial projects orchestrated outside any existing organization the quantity of debt sought is unlikely to be comparable with the value of debt raised by large established corporations.

This is a very simplistic treatment that does not acknowledge the different categories of lender in the debt markets or the numerous debt instruments designed to satisfy particular lender/borrower requirements. However, a potential borrower is more likely to encounter some form of credit rationing rather than progressively increasing rates of interest with additional applications for debt. Furthermore, where interest rates do rise to accommodate increases in the lender's perceived risk, the marginal increases can be small in relation to a manipulated base rate of interest that reflects macroeconomic conditions rather than the entrepreneur's demand for loanable funds. Finally, lending institutions will be influenced by gearing levels and interest cover as much as by the borrower's willingness to pay: the former has immediate implications for the minimum equity requirements of any given entrepreneurial event while the latter is related to achieved profits.

ENTREPRENEURS PREFERENCES.

The principal attractions of debt finance arise from the tax treatment of interest charges, from the reduced requirement for venture evaluation and monitoring expenses and from the non-dilution of control within a private limited company. The first two benefits of debt tend to reduce the aggregate cost of capital employed and, everything else being held equal, gear up the returns of equity investors for given levels of profit. The third benefit of debt arises from the retained autonomy of the entrepreneur and the avoidance of an obligation to distribute entrepreneurial profits to a pure capitalist. These are powerful considerations that make debt a particularly attractive way of funding a venture and, everything else being held equal, would increase the demand for debt and increase the constraints experienced by entrepreneurs who attempt to generate debt. The underlying rationale for the favourable tax treatment of debt charges is difficult to establish and, in view of the preceding discussion, would appear to fall on the inappropriate category of funds.

CONCLUSION

This discussion of the factor market for finance has necessarily avoided a detailed coverage of the many financial instruments and their permutations which may be available. Similarly the impact of economic cycles has also been omitted. It is enough to note that the level of confidence and expectations in upswing will ordinarily reduce any resistance emanating from within the financial sector but, simultaneously, there would be an increased demand for external funds, both debt and equity. The impact on the effective cost of finance would be difficult to establish on *a priori* grounds. In a downswing the situation reverses and typically real interest rates fall, reflecting the apparent, or actual, scarcity of viable propositions combined with a reduced consumer demand for credit. Whereas an increase in the demand for funds can stem from business or private intentions to spend, an endogenous, non-inflationary increase in aggregate spending will originate from business expenditure in the first instance, unless there is a reduction in the propensity of individuals to save which is and is interpreted as a positive signal for the release of strategically withheld entrepreneurial events.

In considering the evolution of an entrepreneurial event from the vision of the individual or group, through the development phase, set up phase, and establishment phase, a number of circumstances can be anticipated where apparent entrepreneurial activity will be constrained by a lack of finance. In addition to a reduction in apparent activity there could follow higher failure rates reflecting a higher level of undercapitalized events than otherwise.

Varying amounts of equity capital will be required but some minimal internal equity is crucial for any entrepreneurial activity. For the potential entrepreneur with no personal wealth it is argued that there is no predictable mechanism for realizing the event. If the vision or concept can not be readily and safely sold on to another entrepreneur with this minimum initial wealth plus an additional increment for the purchase, potential entrepreneurial activity will be lost. The value of internal equity generated by an entrepreneurial team will be ultimately constrained by their private wealth but also by the valuation procedures of the lending institutions. If the practice of these institutions is unrealistically to discount the collateral value of personal assets the entrepreneur will be able to generate less personal liquidity than could otherwise be justified. Whereas the entrepreneur could undertake the task of liquidating private assets personally, there would be an understandable reluctance not just to risk the eventual loss of those personal assets but, in the interim period, to be without the use of those assets whether or not the venture succeeds.

The efficiency and risk aversion of external equity investors directly affects the effective volume of funds available to entrepreneurs. The more unsuccessful external equity investors are at assessing risk, entrepreneurial visions, and entrepreneurial teams, the more inaccessible external equity becomes. In particular, the value of minimum packages of external equity will increase, as will the required rate of return. Those entrepreneurs requiring external equity in smaller amounts than the investors' economic minimum will be constrained, as will those entrepreneurs who anticipate returns substantially exceeding the prevailing rates of interest but which fall short of the target returns of institutional investors. The impact of deficiencies in the market for equity in new private limited companies is multiplied by gearing implications perceived by the suppliers of debt funding. In the case where the equity of a business is exclusively spent on readily saleable assets that are not subject to a liquidators' fraction, every pound of equity could generate a further pound of debt. This is an extreme situation but would set a value for the multiplicative impact of equity.

In the same way as the providers of debt finance can restrict the value of liquidity available to an entrepreneur for their internal investment in equity, so the providers of debt finance can constrain an entrepreneurial event in the set-up and establishment phases of a business if they systematically over discount the value of a business's assets.

Imperfections and anomalies may be present in either the debt or equity markets: the characteristics of imperfection in one market however are not necessarily mirrored in the other market. It must be recognized that from a capital structure perspective, equity can more prudently substitute debt than vice versa and the significance of imperfections in the equity market will have more significant implications than comparable imperfections in the debt market. The significance of this is often lost in the debates and policy concerning finance for new and small firms to the extent that an opposite inference would be drawn from a review of the specific literature. The usual justification for the emphasis on constraints restricting debt generation is based on the prevalence of debt finance and bank borrowing in particular. If debt finance is prevalent whereas external equity is uncommon that would be taken to illustrate the relative significance of the constraints. Imperfections in equity markets would be understated and those in lending markets overstated.

Finally, it must be acknowledged that accurately estimating the sum of funds required to launch an entrepreneurial event for a given level of risk is a most hazardous calculation. In practice the formal calculation is so often found to be erroneous that rule-of-thumb multipliers for the calculated figure can be used by professional assessors. There is a natural reluctance to declare and plan for the uncertainty that exists before the entrepreneurial event is unequivocally self-financing and the origin of this constraint lies as much with the entrepreneur as it does with the financier.

SEVEN

THE FACTOR MARKETS FOR SECONDARY INPUTS

INTRODUCTION

The discussion here focuses on three generic categories of secondary input: plant and machinery, labour, and premises. Distortions in the markets for these inputs which restrict their supply will increase prices and, everything else being equal, increase the amount of finance required to pursue an entrepreneurial event. At the margin, some firms or projects will cease to be viable. Imperfect knowledge and mobility, in a neo-classical sense, will generate sectoral and geographic cameos that need not be mirrored elsewhere in a national economy. The treatment provided here, therefore, is general; its usefulness derives from the applicability to specific and defined contexts.

A feature which distinguishes the inputs referred to above is that they are rarely completely consumed by one commercial operation. Plant and machinery can often achieve a secondhand value that exceeds its scrap value, labour can more or less easily acquire new skills and new employers, and premises typically have useful lives that exceed the requirement of the original owner or tenant. As such, the supply of these inputs is, in part, determined by the demand in previous time periods: the dynamic and cyclical characteristics of an economy can become significant for the combination of resources employed by an entrepreneur and for the categories of entre-preneurial events realized.

PLANT AND MACHINERY

The supply of plant and machinery at any one time is a mixture of new and second-hand equipment. New equipment can be made on a speculative basis and held in stock for future sale or it can be manufactured on a bespoke basis. The more unusual the equipment, the more likely it is that manufacture is to order only. Unique and innovative equipment can be commissioned but similar disadvantages apply to both bespoke and commissioned equipment. There will be long lead times, an increased likelihood of teething problems, no economies of scale or prospect of credit facilities through the supplier.

New equipment manufactured on a speculative basis, that is without the precise identity of the customer being known beforehand, will reflect the market conditions and expectations of future conditions. The determinants of these expectations will be complex and heterogeneous. The buoyancy of the customers' industry will be significant both in terms of capacity requirements and in terms of strategic considerations for the launch of refined or innovative equipment that replaces existing productive capacity. Similarly, competition from other suppliers of plant and machinery will impinge upon trading strategies and tactics.

Under simple neo-classical criteria the decision to invest in plant and machinery is based upon clear and rational rules as to the marginal productivity of the capital and its price *vis-à-vis* the marginal product of the capital which it replaces or labour which can be a substitute. In practice the evaluation procedures of many firms are determined primarily by *ad hoc* and informal mechanisms. While conventional economic criteria should imply the application of some form of discounted cash-flow technique or the calculation of internal rates of return, for many firms, particularly smaller firms, these are not applied. Although the decision may still refer to the expected return on capital employed, this again will often be relegated to a much shorter timespan if the levels of market uncertainty are sufficiently great to make recourse to common pay back rules.

There is a large literature on the decision-making processes of firms about to, or anticipating, purchase of new plant and machinery; it is not relevant to this particular discussion to consider all of these arguments. The main concern here is to contrast the pricing mechanisms which are adopted by those attempting to sell new plant and equipment with the price obtaining on second-hand capital under different economic conditions.

THE SUPPLY OF SECOND-HAND PLANT AND MACHINERY

Second-hand capital is released on to the market in two circumstances. The first describes firms which are upgrading their production process; they release capital on to the second-hand market in order to realize the second-hand value to set against the new investment costs. They are replacing operative but inferior or inappropriate plant and machinery with equipment that is perceived to be superior or more appropriate.

Firms pursuing a strategy that requires upgrading of capital would more probably be found in buoyant industries facing an expanding market, but it could also be the strategy of specific firms that are increasing their market share in a static or declining marketplace since it could be the response of those that face declining markets or market share, and are trying to reverse the condition.

Alternatively firms may release plant and machinery on to the second-hand market because they are reducing the scale of their operation in line with depressed market conditions. In the more extreme case, the shedding of plant and equipment may be associated with company liquidation.

It is accepted that the market for second-hand capital is often highly localized and the shedding of plant and machinery on to such a market may be realized through the sale of equipment at auction. This localized market may therefore be highly volatile and significant in changing the overall pattern of capital available to potential entrepreneurs in that locality. The decision by a firm to shed quantities of second-hand plant and machinery, or the unavoidable release of such plant and equipment due to closure, will necessarily constitute a very large temporary shift in the supply of particular equipment. This may cause a substantial fall in prices when compared to the price level in other parts of the same economy or in immediately preceding time periods.

These two sources of second-hand capital have very different implications. First, firms providing capital as a result of upgrading may attempt to maximize the second-hand price. Indeed, part of the upgrade decision may be based upon an assessment of the mechanism and strategy for achieving a particular price level.

Supplies which arise due to the liquidation of firms on the other hand, are often released on to the market more quickly due to pressures from creditors. As a result, the upgrading of plant and machinery may to some extent achieve second-hand prices that reflect the value of potential output from the displaced machines, while the decline or closure of firms may lead to aberrations in the market that reflect a demand for immediate liquidity. The price of second-hand equipment in this latter case is dislocated from the capitalized value of any future output. There is the potential for a dramatic shift in the price which is not necessarily the outcome of transactions between willing buyers and sellers.

Furthermore, the type and vintage of plant and machinery from the two situations could be expected to differ. Firms releasing plant due to upgrading will have been using that released plant to a growing and often more profitable extent, while the firm which is liquidating assets will more generally have been using those assets to a declining and less profitable extent. While some of this variation in experience may be attributed to managerial differences, when generalized, it could be expected that supplies of capital due to modernization would be from healthier dynamic and growing industries whereas supplies due to liquidation or contraction of firms would tend to refer to declining industries.

The third implication is that given the difference in expected capital releases due to the two main causes cited above, it could be expected that the mixture of second-hand capital would vary according to the rate of change of economic activity. In general it could be expected that periods of relative economic buoyancy would expand the supply from growing industries, while recession would stimulate supply from declining industries that were closing or contracting their operations.

The fourth inference that can be drawn from the potential oscillation of primary sources of second-hand capital relates to the subsequent implications upon economic development. On the one hand, the availability of second-hand plant and machinery in buoyant periods might induce more entrepreneurial activity than otherwise in those sectors that are prosperous and expanding. During depressed conditions, on the other hand, plant and machinery will be available from firms that are contracting or liquidating. Prices achieved for the equipment may drop to very low levels and become attractive to individuals who, without the prospect of secure future employment, view entrepreneurship as the desirable alternative to unemployment.

The former process, which refers to buoyant industries upgrading capital, implies a positive element in the development process as factors of production shift into the industries in which firms are upgrading while the latter case clearly reflects the formation of new businesses in industries where decline has actually caused superficially favourable conditions in terms of the initial financial requirement. The impact of these firms can exacerbate the negative implications of restructuring and reflect the Omega entrepreneurial activity discussed earlier as plant and equipment is temporarily recycled in conditions of post-disturbance cost conditions.

THE SUPPLY OF NEW PLANT AND MACHINERY

Combined with the supply of second-hand equipment must be the dynamic characteristics of the plant and machinery industry itself. Within the industry there will be developments, refinements and completely new innovations. Those firms supplying plant and machinery may themselves be new or established businesses. As previously described, strategic and tactical considerations may determine the appearance of innovative equipment produced by existing firms. The innovative characteristics of the product may determine when a planned launch is likely to be most profitable. Generally, however, similar considerations to those already discussed will prevail: they referred to buoyant and confident industries generating the profit to replace plant and machinery. It is significant that new processes or plant that negotiate economies of scale, for example, or substantially reduce costs of production, may be particularly sought in declining industries when it is calculated that investment is crucial for survival. Under such circumstances innovative plant and machinery may be offered before there are visible signs of industrial recovery or more general economic recovery. In the case of innovative plant and machinery there can be the real prospect of catalytic entrepreneurship being apparent in recessionary or depressed conditions that simultaneously provide potential for allocating applications and a turning point in an economic cycle. New entrants to equipment industries, in contrast, will again be more likely to develop and release new products so as to minimize costs rather than withold launch on strategic grounds.

The capital market facing or confronting new entrepreneurs therefore will be determined, in part, by the rate of change of economic activity in the industry and in the region within which that industry operates.

THE CONTRIBUTION TO DEVELOPMENT

While the above summary itself is brief in terms of its analysis of the capital market, it serves to highlight the main categories and contrasting experiences of capital prices which would be expected to obtain from different sources of plant and equipment, and under different economic conditions. It also enables the analysis to be extended by considering the reaction of different categories of entrepreneur, to the capital market.

Catalytic and allocating entrepreneurs may require new capital or at least an alternative use of second-hand upgrade capital, in order to realize their innovation. Refining and omega entrepreneurs, who are more influenced by the push effect of adverse economic conditions, may be expected to seek out plant and machinery with which they are familiar.

During a period of recession, be it industrial, regional, or in general, it would be expected that a higher proportion of those setting out in business would be pushed by adverse economic conditions. In seeking plant and equipment with which they are familiar, to create their own enterprise, it might be expected that they would refer primarily to the liquidation, closure, or shrinkage supply rather than upgrade capital from growing firms. In the case of buoyant industries, fewer employees would be redundant and therefore find it necessary to consider establishing a new business.

In this sense, in a period of recession, the two supplies of pushed entrepreneurs and second-hand capital from shrinking or liquidated firms, may be very well matched and promote the appearance of refining and omega activity. In the extreme, since the second-hand capital concerned in the period of recession will often derive from the same source as the pushed entrepreneurs, the two may be perfectly matched simply because they are both the outcome of a specific industry or firm's decline or closure.

There is therefore a case for supposing that the development contribution of entrepreneurship may be lower for a given level of apparent activity in a recession and depression than at other phases of an economic cycle. This hypothesis rests upon the argument presented above, that during a period of recession the bulk of second-hand plant and equipment will tend to derive from declining or closing firms, and the bulk of those intending to set up in business will also derive from declining industries and firms. This could indicate a natural tendency for periods of recession to be self-perpetuating: firms setting up in declining industries have an impact that is opposite to that implied by the conventional economic interpretation. These new firms protract and exacerbate the negative affects of restructuring.

There is much evidence to show that the birth rates and closure rates of firms have been rising during the 1970s in the UK. The record levels of births and deaths can be interpreted in two completely different ways. On the one hand a high closure rate reflects the removal of inefficient firms from the production process. The high birth rates represent the transfer of those factors of production to more efficient users. In this sense the high birth and death rates reflect a positive economic restructuring process, as factors of production are reallocated from the less efficient to the more efficient. On the other hand, high closure rates may simply reflect a decline in market demand. The closures occur with a higher incidence of the less efficient, as the more efficient manage to survive, at least in the short term. When released plant and machinery is recycled at very low prices due to the early closures, it may be operated by new omega entrepreneurs giving them a short-term cost advantage. Their operation may indeed undermine the market restricted previously to the surviving and more efficient firms. Under this interpretation, it is the surviving and more efficient firms which are subsequently driven to failure by the competition provided by those firms setting up with the plant and equipment released by the earlier closure of less efficient firms. In terms of economic restructuring this process may be seen as primarily negative.

The omega activity brings forward the decline of an industry in recession and, sooner rather than later, the economic resources employed in the industry will be available for reallocation. The removal of surviving firms due to the impact of omega events may cause a premature removal of the industry, however, rather than its reduction to a more appropriate size. If the economic resources released do not have an immediate, alternative, economic use and lie idle or unemployed following the omega activity the outcome is also negative. Social and economic policy-makers may well see the situation very differently and promote initiatives with conflicting intentions. Similarly, their time horizons will be significant in so far as in the immediate and short term the apparent idleness of resources will be reduced, while in the medium and longer term there will be fewer opportunities.

The implications of this summary of the capital market under fluctuating and different economic conditions is clearly determined by the particular set of entrepreneurs under consideration. As indicated earlier, the incidence of catalytic entrepreneurship would be expected to be lower in periods of recession and higher in periods of economic buoyancy, due to various factors such as strategic considerations of the corporate entrepreneur and the opportunity cost of the employee, who intends to leave salaried employment to pursue an entrepreneurial event. Similarly in a period of recession it is argued that the pattern of plant and equipment available may more strongly reflect disposals from declining industries, rather than the marketing efforts of new capital manufacturers. In a period of recession refining events may be substituted by omega events with no apparent change in entrepreneurial activity at the aggregate level.

In a period of economic buoyancy the opposite might prevail, whereby non-corporate catalytic and allocating entrepreneurs will feel more secure and regard the down-side cost of attempting to innovate their particular ideas as being eroded due to the greater prevalence of alternative employment opportunities. Corporate entrepreneurs will react to the strategic considerations outlined earlier. At the same time, the second-hand capital market will tend to reflect the buoyancy of particular industries in the release of plant and equipment at more realistic prices, due to the upgrading processes of those firms which are profiting from economic upturn. In the case of refining and omega entrepreneurs, periods of economic recession may enable them to attempt to achieve their marginal improvements in efficiency more easily, due to the lower price of plant and equipment from declining industries. In this case such entrepreneurs may, aside from feeling the push pressure of job insecurity or threatened redundancy, also interpret their particular previous employers' experience as being partly due to their employers' managerial inefficiency.

From these arguments it emerges that the relative incidence of realized non-corporate catalytic and allocating entrepreneurship appears to be less likely under conditions of recession when it is most required for future economic developments, and most likely in periods of economic buoyancy.

Finally, in terms of the adjustment process, given catalytic and to some extent allocating improvements in factor allocations, it is also clear that the second-hand capital market, in conjunction with the new capital market, may tend to constitute a resistance to change in the allocation of factors of production. Imperfect market forces could favour an emphasis of factor allocation towards declining sectors in certain circumstances, due to the procedures applied to the disposal of second-hand plant and equipment from liquidating firms. This would appear to impede any process of adjustment towards a more developed or efficient pattern of factor allocation, since it favours those mature or geriatric industries which are least likely to stimulate economic regeneration. Similarly, in a period of economic buoyancy, it might appear that the development process is facilitated by a faster adjustment mechanism, since the second-hand plant and machinery available may promote entrepreneurs to enter industries which are expanding and buoyant.

LABOUR

The labour input considered here excludes the specialized entrepreneurial input and considers any other form of labour with employee or potential employee status: it refers to the profile of the labour market confronting entrepreneurs. The immobility and heterogeneity of labour, combined with its ability to change with education and training, renders the notion of one labour market unrealistic. The entrepreneur will tend to recruit from fragmented and localized markets that are dynamic and not necessarily complete.

There are parallels between labour and capital markets and potential trade-offs between the two categories of input in any resource combination. The non-economic facets of labour, combined with a wider cultural context, however, introduce major difficulties for any analysis that maintains a degree of realism. Furthermore, unlike plant and machinery that is bought with a knowledge of the technical specifications and performance, the capabilities of a particular employee in a particular organization cannot be precisely assessed beforehand. Motivation, morale, and enthusiasm are major determinants of an employee's output, and are situationally determined. The employing organization only partly determines an employee's perceived situation and the entrepreneur or employer has very little or no control over an employee's social situation. As such, successfully recruiting and managing employees requires an aptitude over and above those already alluded to. The contractual basis under which labour may be employed varies significantly within and between economies, as do the statutory obligations of an employer. Finally, it should be noted that a new business in the embryonic stages of its development may rely more on informal networks than acknowledged markets to satisfy its labour requirements.

Acknowledging these points and particularly the use of personal networks to source employees, it follows that networks themselves will be more or less fruitful according to the general characteristics of a population that is available for work. It could be anticipated that beyond the initial growth stages of a new enterprise, personal knowledge of suitable recruits through a network could become inadequate. Substantial difficulties would be anticipated in maintaining a given level of growth in some industries, unless investment in plant and machinery represented a viable alternative to additional labour.

Initial recruits to an emerging enterprise will require a flexibility and dexterity that is not so crucial in established, larger businesses, where specialized functions and systems have been determined. Particular key responsibilities in a new firm do not justify specialized personnel, while the diseconomies of subcontracting operations to consultants, advisors, and suppliers, combined with the potential for a lower level of commitment from external parties, put the non-corporate entrepreneur at a substantial disadvantage. The position is further aggravated by the uncertainty that a potential employee might perceive to be associated with working for a firm that has no track record and offers only the prospect rather than the certainty of being a viable organization. The significance of this uncertainty will be assessed differently by potential employees and may be anticipated to reflect the opportunity cost and transfer earnings of the individual. These factors themselves will reflect economic conditions within particular industries, regions, or the economy as a whole.

Labour becomes available for recruitment as a result of new additions to the labour force, predominantly young adults entering a labour market for the first time, and as a result of employee movements between employers. This latter source of employee is differentiated from the former by virtue of the experience and training acquired in previous occupations. That labour not entering the market for the first time may have done so voluntarily or involuntarily and, whereas there will be circumstances that differentiate every case, there will be generalizations that could be expected to apply under identifiable conditions.

The skill pattern and human capital represented in the labour supply at any one point in time will reflect education and training provision in previous periods and the requirements of previous employers. The qualities of new additions to the labour market will reflect educational policies and social requirements determined by the political process, while displaced labour requiring re-employment will reflect the fortunes of particular industries and the economy more generally. That labour voluntarily making itself available for re-employment is more likely to do so from the retained status of an employee and is unlikely to be generally accessible to a new firm. The conditions referred to earlier that characterize employment opportunities in emerging, new firms, will be unattractive to applicants from more specialized and highly paid occupations and professions, unless compensation for the assumed risk and short-term disbenefit is accommodated in an employment agreement that allows for participation in prospective profits. New entrants to the labour market will by definition have limited experience and ordinarily they will not possess skills that are immediately useful to the establishment of a new enterprise. The opportunity cost of supervision and training will ordinarily outweigh any future benefits.

If these generalizations can be accepted, recruitment will be substantially influenced by the nature and characteristics of that part of a labour force that is involuntarily moving between employers. During the cyclical development of an industry or an economy there are phases where there is an increased probability of this category of labour becoming available.

Firms in buoyant industries that are expanding their operations may release labour, if investment in more capital intensive systems becomes economic at higher levels of output. Labour will be released with skills that are redundant in particular combinations of factor inputs. Other firms in the same industry may react to increasing activity by recruiting additional labour with skills similar to those possessed by their existing employees. The smoothness of any shift from labour to capital throughout an industry cannot be generalized, and will be affected by the volume and value characteristics of incoming investment. Nevertheless, it would ordinarily be the less sophisticated skills that would be replaced by automation. These skills may be useful within the smaller enterprise, although redundant in a previous position.

Industrial recession, on the other hand, will stimulate the release of labour with a broader range of skills that have had particular applications which have become, or are becoming, obsolete. There are no grounds to expect that redundant skills from either a declining or expanding industry will be immediately suitable to other applications that facilitate or fortify the development process. It is the case however, that these skills will be consistent with the requirements of refining and omega activity. The refining and omega entrepreneurs, the plant and machinery, and the labour are simultaneously thrown together to form new enterprises.

Catalytic and allocating entrepreneurial activity which facilitates the development process will not predictably be able to capitalize upon fortuitous circumstances that so neatly marshal the necessary inputs at particular phases of industrial cycles: there becomes the real prospect of skill shortages for the realization of particular entrepreneurial events.

The resulting requirement for reskilling, upgrading, and reorientating of existing skills becomes significant and can be approached from different routes that would reflect varying political standpoints. The significant feature of any process assumed, however, should be the removal of protracted shortages which on the one hand allow the labour with the sought-after skills to establish price premiums, while the unskilled or inappropriately skilled remain unemployed, simultaneously representing an opportunity cost and a depreciating asset from a national perspective. An efficient mechanism to maximize the value of human capital within a working population and a dynamic economy will impinge directly upon the flexibility of the economy as a whole and its performance *inter alia.*

Catalytic and allocating entrepreneurial events require successful input completion in a consistent format. Where the labour force represents a major factor input then an insufficient supply of the appropriate skills will clearly constitute a major constraint upon the ability of that economy to capitalize upon domestic catalytic and allocating entrepreneurial activity.

This factor market is therefore crucial to the adjustment process in development through either catalytic or allocating entrepreneurial activity. It was indicated earlier that the commitment to specific investments may influence the rate of uptake of associated or complementary investments: in a similar, but more significant way, an investment in an economy's human capital can come to represent a constraint on the adoption of new techniques, technologies, and systems if the investment was designed to satisfy specific roles or functions, rather than provide an apparatus to accommodate change. The extent to which the labour force is flexible, and the extent to which retraining facilities exist to adapt it to new requirements, will influence the potential of any economy to become the initiator and beneficiary of entrepreneurial activity.

The main point which emerges, therefore, is that the flexibility of the labour force and the extent to which it is accepted that retraining is a recurrent feature throughout a career will determine in part the ability of the labour market to satisfy an entrepreneurial requirement.

Any mismatch between the rate of change of plant, equipment and systems, and the rate of change of labour skills will determine the ability of an economy to capitalize upon entrepreneurial developments and, simultaneously, the number of entrepreneurial events that transpire to be viable. Where a labour force is inflexible and resistant to new skills, the effective cost of appropriately skilled labour will be higher than otherwise and, everything else being held equal, there will be a stimulus for innovations that are less labour-dependent.

The extent to which there is a legitimate relation between skills, training, and remuneration is not considered here: neither is the responsibility for providing a delivery mechanism. Debates that focus upon the merits of state or industry provision do not acknowledge the almost complete absence of a training market and the prospect of market forces becoming an efficient barometer of dynamic supply and demand conditions. These issues are discussed within a policy context in a later chapter.

LAND AND PREMISES

The factor market for land and premises is potentially the least responsive and most distorted of the secondary input markets: it is characterized by features that do not fit comfortably in a market analysis and in many respects the location, quality, and quantity of commercial and industrial sites are determined as much by political mechanisms as they are by economic ones.

The stock of premises comprises mainly buildings that were designed for clients and uses that have changed or been superseded. New additions to the stock represent a small proportion of the total floor space available. As such the locational and physical characteristics tend to accommodate historical conditions as much as contemporary requirements.

During the realization of an entrepreneurial event there will become a requirement for business premises from which to undertake or base the activity. The variety of requirements and specifications for premises will be as diverse as the events themselves but there are two generalizations that can be anticipated. First, the initial premises required will be small in relation to established business in the same industry, and second, there will be a natural reluctance to accept financial commitments that extend significantly into the future. For the emergent new business without an established customer base there is the prospect of the event being unviable regardless of the planning and market research undertaken beforehand. Under such circumstances buying premises is unlikely to be prudent because of the transaction costs; similarly, long leases that cannot be easily sold on would be unattractive. Both the size and flexibility required by entrepreneurs will, everything else being equal, have implications for diseconomies of scale and experimentation. Furthermore, there will be a deterrent to investment in refurbishment and fittings if all expenditure incurred reverts to the landlord upon termination of any agreement.

It is important to recognize that the factor market for premises cannot be dissociated from the market for land and that the land market itself has peculiarities that set it apart from more conventional economic goods. Land can simultaneously be a public and private good and an investment and consumption good. The heterogeneity of land arises from legal, locational, and physical characteristics. Additionally the land supply is more or less fixed within a national boundary and cannot move between uses at zero cost.

For example land-use planning, and the associated legislation, has evolved in the UK because of these characteristics and subsequently had implications for the responsiveness, or otherwise, of the market. In particular, the premises market can be impeded in any adjustment process by requirements for change-of-use consent or building consent. To compound these considerations are the more mundane factors of the physical processes of building and refurbishing property itself. Time-lags involved for speculators and landlords imply an uncertainty and a hesitation to undertake substantial works that may not be required when complete. Finally, it must be recognized that land is expensive and cannot ordinarily be bought out of current income. The upshot of this is that land rights and buildings are ordinarily purchased after, or immediately prior to, some financial agreement whereby the purchaser raises the requisite funds. The significance of efficient capital markets becomes crucial as does the prospect of macroeconomic policy that impinges upon interest rates and the money supply.

THE SUPPLY OF LAND AND PREMISES

The supply available at any one time is made up of new buildings and buildings that have had previous uses. New building can be undertaken on a speculative or bespoke basis: it can be undertaken with a view to purchase by the final user or purchase by an intermediary who anticipates selling-on or renting to the end user. The supply of new building is initially determined by the availability of suitable sites and that is very much determined by planning legislation. The granting of planning permission confers a premium on development sites over and above alternative use values such that supply is very much determined by planning authorities rather than free market forces. The planning machinery does respond to demand for premises but it also reflects wider social and political considerations. The availability of new premises is unlikely to impinge on the requirements of new firms directly unless the buildings are to be rented subsequently or to be leased by an intermediary. New buildings bought by existing firms do imply older premises becoming available that would not otherwise have done so.

Restrictions on the supply of development land and the minimum standards of construction will, everything else being held equal, inflate the price of industrial and commercial property. Also significant however will be the prevailing rate of interest. Because the combined cost of land and construction are high, purchase is made following the acceptance of some form of debt that is typically discharged over medium or long terms. The cost and therefore demand for new buildings will be determined by prevailing interest levels.

The release of existing premises on to the market will reflect in part the availability and cost of new, more suitable buildings. Also it will reflect the fortunes of the economy or particular regions and industries. In depressed conditions it could ordinarily be anticipated that the availability of premises would ease as some firms are liquidated or contracted. In practice the link may not be so direct. Mature and established firms can have the assets to finance a series of losses through economic downturn and may reduce operations while not releasing surplus property space on to the market. The costs of relocating in terms of physical removal and installation and lost output can greatly exceed the costs of maintaining surplus space. A larger firm in a declining industry could strategically manage closure to minimize losses and realize more acceptable prices for the plant and equipment released. The release of premises would be the final disposal and may occur months or years after the recession which prompted the winding-up.

The space released under these conditions is unlikely to be immediately suitable for new and embryonic businesses. Rather, there would be a role for speculators or entrepreneurial developers, if sites released in this way are to supplement the stock of premises suitable for smaller firms. Significant time-lags could be expected with such projects and the appearance of converted space could follow substantially after the final disposal of the original occupier.

Smaller businesses and firms adversely affected by recessionary conditions will not have the momentum of the larger counterparts and the premises will become available for sale or reletting more promptly. An elementary observation, however, is that the rate of new firm starts cannot exceed the rate of small firm closures if this is the only source of supply: the stock of small firms would be constant under such conditions but the character of the stock could change, reflecting the predominance of particular categories of entrepreneur. Consistent with the inferences drawn earlier, the prospect of refining and omega entrepreneurs encountering factor market constraints in recession is small.

During recovery and boom conditions existing small firms prospering from the more buoyant conditions might be expected to require additional space. This can be achieved by relocating in larger premises and thus incurring the costs of moving and lost output. Alternatively, the effective area of the original premises can sometimes be extended as a feasible alternative. In practice the flexibility within given operating areas for ranges of output can be substantial. Shift systems and investment in fixtures and fittings to utilize available space more efficiently are obvious examples. Certainly, there is not likely to be an immediate relation between economic upturn and the demand for larger premises. In addition to the substantial costs involved in moving and the scope for increased output from a given space, increasing sales on the other hand can have implications for working capital requirements that have adverse affects on cash flow and the ability to finance additional capital expenditures. The decision to relocate in larger premises will more probably reflect a dynamic firm that has been increasing turnover and market share and is confident that the growth path can be maintained irrespective of more general economic cycles.

THE DEMAND FOR LAND AND PREMISES

The demand for land and premises suitable for embryonic businesses will be represented by intermediaries and, to a lesser extent, entrepreneurs themselves. Clearly the demand from intermediaries will reflect the perceived demand of entrepreneurs willing and able to rent or lease the units. This introduces the prospect of time-lags in addition to those emanating from the factors already discussed. Periods of recession may be conducive to the activities of these intermediaries and speculative landlords. Inflationary periods may similarly induce activity if the investment is seen as a way of maintaining real value or generating capital gain in addition to the anticipated income stream from leasing or renting.

The demand from potential tenants for smaller units is clearly a derived demand and particularly low costs are unlikely to induce more new businesses than would otherwise be emerging. High property prices, however, and associated high rents will reduce the viability of new firms at the margin and affect the number of entrepreneurial events that are successfully realized. Property-based taxes will, in the absence of other distortions, have a similar impact as artificially high prices.

Clearly the property market is highly localized and the viability of an area or region introduces social and cultural aspects to the debate. Also important is the supporting infrastructure represented by road and rail links, proximity to sea and airports, and the availability of other inputs. The significance of regional and land-use legislation and the prevalence of economic externalities which have engendered this political reaction, combined with the significance of macroeconomic policy upon interest rates particularly, and investment confidence generally, all have impacts upon the allocation of existing premises between actual and prospective occupants. The costs of relocating and the difficulty of marginally adjusting occupied areas to suit economic conditions, combined with the elasticity that exists in practice with regard to the intensity of use of particular premises, all suggest that the use of available industrial and commercial space is not as efficient as possible and that the costs of space are higher than they would be with no official policies to internalize perceived externalities.

SUMMARY

The generic groups of secondary inputs isolated in this chapter have particular facets that prohibit definitive comment. Every local, regional, and industrial sector will present particular anomalies and exceptions to any generalizations. Nevertheless, these secondary input markets cannot be avoided in most cases of entrepreneurial activity. In part, the appearance of entrepreneurial events will reflect the opportunities to marshal particular combinations of resources within predetermined budget constraints. There is unlikely to be only one combination of resources that will achieve an entrepreneurial vision: rather there is scope for trade-offs between particular inputs and for the acceleration or retardation of activity to capitalize upon the opportunistic acquisition of available inputs.

The effective cost and supply of land and labour in particular are influenced by the social and political mechanisms within a national boundary as much as by the economic system. Oscillations can be detected in the non-economic systems as well as in the general level of an economy's activity. These fluctuations will themselves impinge upon costs and attitudes and affect the apparent levels and characteristics of entrepreneurial activity at the macro level. The discussion presented of the generic secondary input markets serves to highlight those features of imperfect knowledge, imperfect mobility and heterogeneity that frustrate the practical application of neo-classical analyses while suggesting that the economic condition in one time period will impinge upon the level and category of entrepreneurial activity in a subsequent period and that those entrepreneurial events actually realized will have an impact upon entrepreneurial visions that are viable in the immediate future.

THE FACTOR MARKET SYNTHESIS

The preceding observations on factor markets and their impact upon economic conditions confronting entrepreneurs can be combined to present a relatively simple and clear conclusion. In summary it appears that new and small firms may have a negative restructuring effect in periods of recession, and a positive one in those of recovery and buoyancy. The underlying causes of these phenomena reside in the variations in factor market conditions which naturally occur according to the rate of change in the markets concerned.

NEGATIVE RESTRUCTURING

Given the arguments above it is sensible to assume that in a period of recession in any given product market, there will be a natural tendency for new firms to set up in that market if entry to alternative and more buoyant alternatives is prohibited by a lack of both appropriate skills and relatively low-cost plant and equipment.

In a condition of general recession this trend is emphasized, since the supplies of entrepreneurs, labour, and plant and equipment, will have a higher probability of originating from declining industries: new and small firms will contribute little to a positive reallocation of resources; rather, they will tend to have a negative effect through omega events which recycle factors of production in short-term cost conditions which may actually undermine the viability of those efficient firms which have survived the downturn in market conditions.

This is not to suggest a general conclusion in all senses, since the natural attributes of small firms in terms of their flexibility when confronting new conditions, provide them with a comparative advantage over larger and more established suppliers. The salient observation here is that these advantages will be less effective in terms of a positive reallocation of factor inputs. The majority effect will be destructuring rather than restructuring since efficient enterprise may be undermined in the short term, thus preventing medium and longer term survival.

POSITIVE RESTRUCTURING

Where particular product markets are buoyant, a very different process would be expected. The supply of new entrants will confront dramatically different conditions in terms of factor markets, and their own characteristics and motivations would also contrast those of entrants in a period of recession.

Those setting up under these circumstances will tend to be attracted for the positive reasons of catalytic, allocating, or refining potential rather than omega recycling.

In a condition of general economic recovery and buoyancy it would be expected that a more general positive restructuring effect is realized. The aforementioned characteristics of flexibility in small firms when confronting changing economic conditions of a positive nature will lead to a higher probability that they cause positive restructuring. Those attracted into enterprise will create the labour skills and plant and equipment requirements necessary for the success of their visions without the distraction of cheaper inputs since these will be inappropriate to their needs.

Again, it must be stressed that this is not a general rule but rather a case of relative probabilities. The entrepreneurial content of new and small firms will tend to vary according to the rate of economic change in general, the rate within specific industrial sectors, and, due to their spatial distribution, there will be variations between different regions.

EIGHT
ENTREPRENEURSHIP AND ECONOMIC CYCLES—A SYNTHESIS

Finally, in this section on factor market analysis, it is necessary to examine more closely some macroeconomic implications of the micro approach adopted in previous chapters. Much of the preceding argument utilizes the notion of categories of entrepreneurship, as indicated by their relative content of Schumpeterian entrepreneurial activity. Since Schumpeter developed this concept in order to explain economic development and cyclical activity at a macroeconomic level, it is incumbent upon the authors to explore the differences from his explanation which their analysis implies. This requires some repetition and a much closer examination of Schumpeter's proposals in order to place differences and alterations in interpretation in context. The purpose of this chapter, therefore, is to explore further the role of entrepreneurship in cyclical economic activity given the observations established in earlier chapters.

It is assumed throughout that a crude proxy measure for economic activity would be the value of production or gross national product. No attempt is made to review the many major theoretical contributions which have been postulated over the decades to explain cycles in economic activity. Similarly, it is not our task to undertake an empirical enquiry into the nature of periodicity in the case of such cycles, indeed our analysis must begin by presenting an argument against their natural occurrence.

THE CASE AGAINST CYCLES

For a variable to be termed cyclical, it is insufficient for it merely to fluctuate through time. The fact that there is an identifiable cycle in the fluctuations which the variable experiences implies an element of regularity, a distinct periodicity, and therefore some predictability. Many of the arguments presented above, however, would tend to support the view that entrepreneurship will lead to relatively smooth, non-cyclical changes in economic activity.

A case was made in Chapter 2 for the application of Catastrophe Theory at a conceptual level, in order to justify the claim that economic development through catalytic entrepreneurship would tend to retain a strong stochastic element. This argument can now be extended in order to demonstrate why, in theory at least, it might be expected that cyclical or regular periodic movements in economic development will not tend to occur.

The catalytic entrepreneurial event is seen to be conceived due to the gradually increasing input of knowledge to a given stock of imagination, i.e. at some point, as the information content rises, there is a change in the equilibrium condition, or in this case the general mode of operation, that cannot be traced backwards, in gradualistic steps, to the previous methods which obtained. This can be regarded as a catastrophic event. As indicated in previous discussions, this terminology implies a pejorative element which is inappropriate, but is retained since it refers to an identifiable theoretical approach. This theoretical structure is clearly over-simplified, however, since it would be expected that the stock of imagination and the pattern of imagination would vary through time rather than being fixed. Similarly information will not tend to be accumulated in a smooth, continuous fashion, but will itself tend to vary as information is both combined and extended. The model is still useful, however, since it does identify the major inputs required for the conception of potential catalytic entrepreneurial events. If it is further assumed that there are no obstructions to the realization of catalytic entrepreneurial ideas, then the case for a smooth pattern of economic development can be made.

Catalytic entrepreneurial events would be expected to occur in a random manner, in different regions and different industries. As communications between regions and between industries improve, it would be expected that there be a more rapid interflow and exchange of information, both throughout those regions and industries and between them. This has clear implications. Increasingly, individuals within one industry will be aware of information which has been developed or discovered in a different, entirely disparate industry. The information received has resulted from the efforts of other individuals or groups of individuals, who were pursuing entirely different ends from those which preoccupy the recipients in the industry concerned. While deterministic forces are naturally strong in the pursuit of information to solve specific problems, these stochastic elements in information exchange will be more influential as communication processes improve.

Given the assumption, for the present, of no obstacles to the realization of entrepreneurial events, it would be expected that this flow of information would facilitate the development process, and probably generate a smoother pattern of catalytic entrepreneurial events within each industry and region.

The relative frequency of catalytic entrepreneurial events within different industries may vary, as would their significance or impact on those particular industries. Some industries might experience a large number of relatively minor catalytic events, while others experience fewer but more significant changes. Industries also differ in terms of their flexibility and the time period which must ensue for the innovation of catalytic entrepreneurial events. This flexibility would vary, not only according to the relative impact or significance of the entrepreneurial event concerned within a specific industry, but also between industries for catalytic events of a comparable and similar significance. The specific flexibility would reflect the variations in plant and equipment used, attitudinal characteristics in different sectors and the minimum practical times required for adjustment.

These points when taken together present a picture of increased entrepreneurial activity at a catalytic level, due to improved communication processes and information exchange. This picture would also depict different industries as changing at different rates, according to different types of entrepreneurial event, and also because of different periods in their plant and equipment upgrading and adjustment.

Viewed at an aggregate level, therefore, the picture would be one of smooth economic development with a secular trend which was generally upward, given continual improvements in information exchange between industries and regions. There is no indication, given the assumptions that have been made, that a natural tendency for a cyclical pattern will emerge. Indeed the points made, and the coincidence of different industrial patterns of change in different stages of the innovation of entrepreneurial events, would tend to suggest a stable pattern of development around a secular improvement in economic activity rather than cyclical activity.

Despite the above arguments, it is accepted that identifiable cycles do exist in practice. This therefore leaves open the question as to the role which entrepreneurial events might play in the generation and perpetuation of such cyclical activity.

First consider the original explanation proposed by Schumpeter in his theory of economic development[1] and which he expanded upon and substantiated in more detail in *Business Cycles*.[2] We focus our attention, primarily, on the theory of economic development since it is the developmental context rather than the empirical validation of cycles which is most pertinent to our arguments.

A SUMMARY OF SCHUMPETER'S ARGUMENT

Schumpeter also argues that there is a need to consider the entrepreneurial contribution to cycles in economic activity from a starting point of stability. He points out that if entrepreneurial events occurred continually through time, then it would be expected that economic development would also follow a smooth course. He goes on to observe that economic development is not smooth, but that it is obstructed by crises which interrupt the development process. He indicates that these obstructions occur frequently, but also in a periodic way which implies a cyclical rather than a random process. He also argues that the obstructions or setbacks which occur are permanent and that they arrest the development process which, once it is reasserted, starts from a different position with different individuals involved. There is not a gradual process of development. He cites the analogy of a tree growing and branching out. Branches which have been hindered do not continue to grow as they would have done.

A question which preoccupies much of his analysis refers to the extent to which economic variables alone may be responsible for these crises, as they are called, or disturbances in the process of economic development. Clearly many of the incidents which can be classified as crises are exogenous to the economic system. A number of different events are cited as examples of exogenous influences which would be expected to disturb the development process. It is also clear that the crises envisaged can be both demand- or supply-side in nature. Since crises would appear, in this format, to have strong stochastic and exogenous elements, Schumpeter argues that no complete economic theory can be ascribed to the explanation of the disturbances which they cause.

This is not to say that no attempt should be made to identify the economic elements within the cyclical process. The implication of much of Schumpeter's argument is that in the absence of exogenous, random, or stochastic shocks, there would still be a cyclical pattern in economic development. He argues that certain elements within the total set of crises that occur do appear to be part of a wavelike process of change, and therefore economic theory does have a question to answer as to why smooth development would not naturally occur even in the absence of exogenous shocks to the system.

Schumpeter ascribes three classes of event in the economic process of development: first, the circular flow of economic activity; second, the development activity generated by entrepreneurs; and third, obstructions to the development process which take the form of a cyclical pattern.

His analysis proceeds to describe the entrepreneurial role in the cyclical process, explain it, and then to consider some of the consequences for the development process.

One of the first points to emerge in this train of argument is that booms lead naturally to depression in economic conditions, and depression leads naturally to boom. Schumpeter argues that booms naturally lead to depression because the booms consist of a cluster or swarm of entrepreneurial events which so displace the equilibrium conditions operating hitherto that many firms are also displaced from the process, and there is a painful period of adjustment which may involve the reallocation of factors of production, particularly labour. This will lead to, or be interpreted as, a depression. The depression arises in a sense from the adjustment process due to the boom effect of clustered entrepreneurial events.

Part of the analysis which Schumpeter uses to explain why depression may cause booms is reminiscent in the context of the arguments put forward earlier, since the points made can be interpreted in the context of factor market analysis. To quote part of Schumpeter's argument:

> One favourable circumstance, which always facilitates and partly explains a boom, must be particularly remembered, namely the state of affairs created by every period of depression. As is well known, there are generally masses of unemployed, accumulated stocks of raw materials, machines, buildings, and so forth offered below cost of production, and there is as a rule an abnormally low rate of interest.[3]

Schumpeter argues, however, that these natural relationships within booms or slumps which can be interpreted as leading to further booms or slumps are not relevant to the main objective of his coverage, which is to identify the role of entrepreneurs in causing the booms and slumps in the first place. The assumption as indicated above is that from a steady state booms and slumps would tend to occur naturally. The associated conditions which might perpetuate the process do not explain how it is originally caused; hence they are not given further coverage explicitly in Schumpeter's theory.

THE REINFORCEMENT OF CYCLES

Schumpeter also considers three circumstances which will tend to augment the effect of the swarming process in terms of entrepreneurial events. Here the concern is not with identifying factors causing the swarming or clustering, but merely those factors which, given the clustering, tend to emphasize the impact upon economic activity.

The first of these is significant to our analysis since it refers to one of the variables in Schumpeter's argument, which will be adjusted fundamentally in the modified arguments which are to follow.

> The vast majority of new combinations will not grow out of the old firms or immediately take their place, but appear side by side and compete with them.[4]

The point here is that where such swarms or clusters of entrepreneurial events occur, a vast number of established firms are affected. They may either settle to a smaller size, they may adjust their own market position, or they may go bankrupt and cease trading. Any of these reactions by established firms to the setting up of new firms which embody the entrepreneurial activity will cause a realignment in the allocation of the factors of production, and obviously the more firms which are affected by this adjustment process the more marked it will be in terms of the overall level of economic activity.

A second characteristic of the clustering process which will also tend to increase its impact on the overall level of economic activity refers to what Schumpeter describes as the secondary wave of effects which are set off by the primary wave of entrepreneurial actions. Possibly one of the simplest ways of describing these processes is to liken them to multiplier effects on demand, and accelerator effects on investment.

The impact of the primary wave of entrepreneurial actions is followed by the introduction of competitive innovation by non-entrepreneurs in Schumpeter's terms, who spread the original new idea or combination throughout the circular flow as dictated and constrained by commercial conditions. The point here is that, as they innovate the new techniques, so they cause multiplier effects by creating purchasing power for those that they employ, and they also cause, in turn, accelerator effects on investment to support the higher level of demand caused by the multiplier effect.

The third circumstance which increases the impact of swarms of entrepreneurs upon aggregate economic activity refers to the errors in judgement which may be made by existing businesses. Again there is no *a priori* reason why errors should not be disbursed evenly through time. From this starting point, however, it is clear that unpredicted entrepreneurial swarms will tend to jeopardize the decision-making processes of established businesses, where these decisions refer to the time immediately prior to the initial appearance of the entrepreneurial events. The errors which occur as a result of this inability to predict change may then be compounded by further errors in their reaction to change. Their perception of the threat to their own trading conditions will almost certainly be inaccurate. Schumpeter argues that that perception will often be more gloomy than is actually necessitated in practice. As a result, there is the potential for large groups of firms to have expectations and make decisions on the basis of them, which are all incorrect but the incorrectness is, in a sense, consistent. Examples such as speculative booms which subsequently collapse, and over-production as a result of such activity, are used to substantiate these arguments.

THE CLUSTERING PROCESS

The identification of these circumstances serves to interpret and describe the cyclical effect. Having assumed the clustering process of entrepreneurial events or entrepreneurs, Schumpeter then goes on to explain why such clustering occurs in practice.

> Why do entrepreneurs appear, not continuously, that is singly in every appropriately chosen interval, but in clusters? Exclusively because the appearance of one or a few entrepreneurs facilitates the appearance of others, and these the appearance of more, in ever increasing numbers.[5]

As has already been indicated in Chapter 2, this whole thesis rests upon the notion of a natural resistance to change within the circular flow. Schumpeter refers frequently to the role of the 'pioneer' entrepreneur. He argues that entrepreneurship requires leadership in order to break down the natural barriers to its emergence. In the limiting case, following a period completely devoid of entrepreneurial activity, there is considerable resistance to potential entrepreneurial events. The 'pioneer' entrepreneur is the person who first succeeds in achieving an entrepreneurial breakthrough. In so doing, this entrepreneur reduces the resistance to subsequent events, and thus makes the task of introducing further entrepreneurial events easier. Following the success of the 'pioneer' entrepreneur, lesser entrepreneurs are able to succeed because lower obstacles confront them. With successive entrepreneurial breakthroughs the obstacles and resistance are reduced almost entirely, and with their reduction the level of entrepreneurship which can succeed may be very low. As this process continues the levels of entrepreneurship required are reduced and must eventually approximate to zero. This 'dam-burst'-like process would be expected to have large secondary-wave effects of the type described above, in terms of the three circumstances used to associate swarms of entrepreneurship with large changes in the level of economic activity and subsequent depression.

There is, however, no apparent justification in Schumpeter's explanation for the claim that these appearances will, in his words, be 'in ever increasing numbers'. It would appear from the argument, that entrepreneurial activity would cease as the obstacles, once completely broken down, enable all commercially viable entrepreneurial events to occur.

The question which then remains is why entrepreneurial events do not occur in an even distribution through time, since barriers to their inception have been removed. Schumpeter argues that over and above the natural tendency for booms to lead to depression due to the adjustment process, the new equilibrium, once attained, will itself constitute a natural source of resistance to further entrepreneurial events, and therefore the process of entrepreneurial accumulation will begin again until the next pioneering entrepreneur breaks through the resistance and thus facilitates the realization of another cluster or swarm of entrepreneurial occurrences.

Many of the observations of this particular section of Schumpeter's analysis are less relevant to the experiences of the late twentieth century, since they refer to instances of price reduction and very low interest rates, alongside other economic conditions which are not readily observable in the 1980s. Other observations which are made are more relevant to the present analysis and do merit careful consideration.

COUNTERCYCLICAL INFLUENCES

Schumpeter argues that the relatively sharp fluctuations in economic activity which the swarming of entrepreneurial events would appear to imply may be smoothed out naturally due to the different characteristics of new, as opposed to established, firms. If large numbers of entrepreneurial events did occur in the manner predicted, and large numbers of established firms were affected significantly and very quickly, then clearly the aggregate level of economic activity would be seen to react very sharply. This effect would be compounded by the other circumstances which Schumpeter associated with the clustering of entrepreneurial events, i.e. the secondary waves of innovation and the investment effects which they cause, along with the coincidence of errors operating in the same direction in existing firms. It would appear therefore from Schumpeter's own analysis that these compounding factors, when combined with the swarming effect of entrepreneurs, must have a dramatic effect upon the level of economic activity. The main observations which tend to mitigate against such sharp fluctuations refer first to the type of firm and its relative ability to resist economic conditions.

When referring to the impact of economic adjustment upon firms which is necessitated by the onset of entrepreneurial change, Schumpeter states:

> Within every industry new enterprises are generally implicated considerably more than established businesses, which seems to contradict our interpretation. This is to be explained as follows: an old business has the buffer quasi rent, and, what is more important, generally accumulated reserves. It is embedded in protecting relationships, often effectively supported by banking connections of many year's standing. It may be losing ground for years without its creditors becoming uneasy. Therefore it holds out much longer than a new enterprise, which is strictly and suspiciously scrutinised, which has no reserves but at best only overdraft facilities, and which only needs to give a sign of embarrassment to be considered as a bad debtor. Hence, the reaction of the change in all conditions upon new enterprises may become visible earlier and more strikingly than that upon old businesses.[6]

This observation that more established firms will actually be better able to resist changing circumstances than newer ones, helps to explain why the sharpness of fluctuations in aggregate economic activity may be reduced. It also implies a natural process by which the causes of changing conditions, in the form of new firms, may refer to those most at risk to the adjustment process. Thus the impact of change is reduced as the innovation process is slowed down.

Schumpeter goes further and points out that bankruptcy is itself often a slow process, and that although the causes of it may have been sown in the period of boom, when new alternative products and processes are first innovated by entrepreneurs, the established firm may survive the recession and depression which follows, and only cease trading as a new boom is in process. He describes the results of this very impressively as follows: 'So that the drowning takes place in sight of dry land.'[7]

The final observation in terms of a moderating influence upon fluctuations in economic conditions is covered in the very short section which Schumpeter devotes to the policy implications of his theory. The observation which he makes about large firms and governments is useful in explaining a reduced impact on cyclical activity. He points out that large companies, and also governments, will better understand the cyclical process which is outlined and therefore begin to anticipate it. As a result they will resist investments in construction and the purchase of new plant and equipment and new projects, if they perceive a depression as being the next stage of the cycle. He therefore argues that the full impact of changing technology will not occur suddenly, but will be delayed or postponed until economic conditions appear more favourable for its introduction. Given this summary of Schumpeter's view we can now consider how it would be modified in the light of more modern conditions.

SOME ADJUSTMENTS TO SCHUMPETER'S INTERPRETATION OF THE BUSINESS CYCLE

There are two major changes to the interpretation which Schumpeter has proposed which are appropriate. The first of these refers to the role of new businesses and entrepreneurship and the second, which follows from it, refers to the crucial role of the 'pioneer' entrepreneur as depicted by Schumpeter.

THE ROLE OF NEW ENTERPRISE

Schumpeter reveals at several points his belief that entrepreneurial events are primarily the responsibility of new enterprises and new businesses. Consider the following:

> In one sense, he (the entrepreneur) may indeed be called the most rational and the most egotistical of all. For, as we have seen, conscious rationality enters much more into the carrying out of new plans, which themselves have to be worked out before they can be acted upon, than into the mere running of an established business, which is largely a matter of routine. And the typical entrepreneur is more self-centred than other types, because he relies less than they do on tradition and connection and because his characteristic task—theoretically as well as historically—consists precisely in breaking up old, and creating new, tradition.[8]

> First of all, there is the dream and the will to found a private kingdom, usually, though not necessarily, also a dynasty. The modern world really does not know any such positions, but what may be attained by industrial or commercial success is still the nearest approach to medieval lordship possible to modern man.[9]

Finally, to refer again to a later section in Schumpeter's theory where he commits himself to regarding entrepreneurship as being almost synonymous with new business for the purposes of understanding his particular theory.

> We can best elucidate the nature of the operation, however, if we assume that all innovations are embodied in newly established businesses, are financed solely by newly created purchasing power, and take their place beside businesses which belong strictly to the circular flow and work without profit, and which, therefore, in consequence of the increase in their costs, begin to produce at a loss.[10]

The significance of these points emerges if one considers the constraints upon new firm formation and new individual entrepreneurial attempts as identified in earlier chapters, particularly in the case of entrepreneurship and finance.

It has been argued in preceding chapters that the individual entrepreneur will face the most monumental of tasks when attempting to realize a particular new idea. In a sense they are least well placed as far as the probability of a successful result is concerned. The movement by an entrepreneur, or a potential entrepreneur, between the conception of a particular idea and the production of a first prototype, for example, requires considerable resources of both finance and time. Indeed, the information required to conceive entrepreneurial events at the forefront of technology in the 1980s would be very difficult for any individual to accumulate, retain, and manipulate successfully in order to present a viable idea. Furthermore, the development of the product from a first prototype to a commercial supply will often incur considerable costs requiring particular financial 'packaging'.

This process also requires the entrepreneur to manipulate several different markets successfully as both Say and Leibenstein emphasize in the input completion role.

Finally, once the new enterprise is operational it will encounter additional financial requirements. As Schumpeter himself claims, new businesses face a more difficult task in terms of attracting finance, even though they themselves may be better placed, in actuality, to do so.

> That firm which is well supported, and not the one that is most perfect in itself, has the best chance of surviving a crisis.[11]

Two major points emerge from the above.

The first of these refers to the information required for entrepreneurial breakthroughs in an age of rapid technological change in many disparate areas, and rapid communications between those areas. In this situation it is increasingly unlikely that any one individual would be in a position, as indicated earlier, to apply the information required for an entrepreneurial breakthrough on their own. It is for this reason that many breakthroughs are often associated with teams of researchers, for example, either within large corporations, within research units in different sciences, or within medium-sized companies who have pursued a specific problem in a determined manner.

The second point refers to the difficulties which the attempted acquisition of funds for an entirely new venture would be expected to experience. Access to funds for product development, prototype analysis, market research, and final commercial exploitation will tend to be biased towards established firms rather than individuals. Exceptions which might be argued to prove this rule tend to draw attention, in some senses, misleadingly in so far as those individuals who do succeed represent major personal achievement but minor impact upon the economy as a whole.

For these reasons, entrepreneurial events in a high-technology age of rapid and improving communications may be concentrated more frequently in established firms and larger corporations. This does not detract from their impact upon Schumpeter's notion of a circular flow, neither does it reduce the cogency of most of the arguments which have been put forward, both in terms of Schumpeter's analysis and that of others. It simply means that the synonymity between entrepreneurship and individual effort should be rejected in favour of a more cross-fertilization-based approach involving synergy between individuals operating in groups.

THE 'PIONEER' RECONSIDERED

This reconstructed image of the entrepreneur or the producers of entrepreneurial events also has implications for Schumpeter's notion of the 'pioneer' entrepreneur. There is now no longer a need for a single entrepreneur to commence the 'dam-bursting' operation of breaking down resistance to entrepreneurial events. Large corporations, and indeed medium-sized firms will have sufficient financial and informational resources to undertake entrepreneurial events if they feel they are commercially viable. The notion of an individual entrepreneur leading, therefore, to a swarm of entrepreneurial followers in disparate fields and areas of production is also inappropriate. There is no reason why the entrepreneurial actions of one company will necessitate many other companies to present entrepreneurial events in other unrelated areas. The swarming of entrepreneurs in disparate areas is no longer justified, since the nature of the obstructions which Schumpeter refers to has been changed. There is no longer a common resistance to change which, once overcome by the 'Pioneer', is successively eroded by entrepreneurs in diverse industries.

SCHUMPETER'S THEORY IN A CONTEMPORARY WORLD

The above changes in Schumpeter's model do not necessitate a complete departure from his perception of the entrepreneurial contribution to cycles in economic activity. It is possible to argue that entrepreneurial events of this kind may still be concentrated periodically through time. Much of the secondary-wave activity to which Schumpeter refers would then follow in the same way.

The major new requirement in terms of explanation refers to the replacement of the 'pioneer' entrepreneur by some theory which demonstrates how large and established firms might decide to release catalytic entrepreneurial events at the same time, or in a very short space of time. The point here is that there is no clear relationship between the generation of a viable catalytic entrepreneurial event within a firm, and the time at which it is first presented to the marketplace.

This point refers back to that made by Schumpeter when considering moderating influences upon the operation of the cycle. He observed that governments and, in this case, established firms in particular would begin to learn how cycles operated and therefore judge their investment activity accordingly. If this observation is simply extended to include the release of catalytic entrepreneurial events, then we have a model for explaining how such events might be clustered without requiring the services of a 'pioneer' entrepreneur. Established firms release catalytic entrepreneurial ideas and events when they judge the economic climate to be most suitable and conducive to success.

The major problem with this reinterpretation of events is that it does not explain how the economic climate improves to the point where catalytic entrepreneurial events are released. The same criticism which Schumpeter levelled at the reliance upon the secondary wave of events and associated changes for the generation of cycles applies here. One way of reconciling the problem is to differentiate between individual catalytic entrepreneurs and corporate entrepreneurs, and to start from the economic condition characterized by stability and equilibrium.

In this situation reliance would be placed primarily upon individual catalytic entrepreneurial events. If it was assumed that the corporate sector has a propensity to release their 'in-house' catalytic events once economic conditions are seen to be improving, i.e. the level of economic activity is increasing, then they could be assumed, at the limit, to retain such events given a depressed or static economic environment. This reintroduces the role of the 'pioneer' entrepreneur in a slightly different form. In this case it is not a pioneer event which causes a dam to burst, it is the operation or success of a single catalytic entrepreneur which creates the potential for allocating activity and further innovation to take place. In turn this creates the conditions that release corporate catalytic entrepreneurship, not because it has been held back by any forms of social resistance to change, but simply because of the strategic decisions taken within existing organizations. Once economic activity begins to grow, then corporate catalytic entrepreneurial events will tend to be released, the potential for allocating activity expands disproportionately and a boom will develop.

This particular vision of the cycle also requires some analysis of turning points, as well as an explanation of cumulative upswings and downswings.

The upper turning point can be explained by the coincidence of a number of different factors. The first and most significant would arise from the diminution of the stock of strategically withheld events. The gestation period of a catalytic event can be accelerated or retarded by the host firm within certain limits only. Once those events researched and developed for market have been released there will be a very reduced number of embryonic events that can be brought forward fast enough for release in boom conditions. The natural reduction over time in the rate of appearance of new catalytic events would reduce the opportunities for allocating entrepreneurs and ultimately there would appear diminishing marginal returns from the effort of allocators as the flow of catalytic events ceased completely.

An additional brake in boom conditions, that may be more or less significant in specific economies, would be supply-side bottlenecks caused by the employment of more marginal factors of production. The impact of cost increases due to the scarcity of skilled labour, premises, and appropriate plant and equipment would be expected to cause firms to experience a reduction in their ability to sustain expansion or achieve viability for new projects.

Once the upper turning point had been passed, then recession would be explained again by a number of coincidental characteristics. The first of these is that the number of catalytic entrepreneurial events would be reduced at the limiting case to zero, as corporations would no longer have any events to withhold. Any potential catalytic events which were generated by existing organizations in this period would be developed more slowly or held back by the firms in anticipation of economic recovery which would facilitate successful commercial realization and innovation. The second characteristic of recession would be a lower incidence of allocating entrepreneurship, as the potential for viable innovation has been reduced, and diminishing marginal returns referred to above are experienced more widely. Third there would be a greater incidence of refining entrepreneurial activity in terms of attempts to reduce levels of inefficiency within traditional forms of factor allocation. Finally there would be the emergence of the omega entrepreneur as a special case, leading to a short-term, self-perpetuating decline. Plant, equipment, and labour is recycled to omega-type entrepreneurs at prices less than the cost of production, allowing these new firms temporarily to undercut the prices of established firms.

The lower turning point could be achieved in this model by any one, or combination, of three influences. First, in economies with a significant industry or sector devoted to the design and manufacture of plant, machinery, and equipment, there is the real prospect of catalytic events being released according to a strategic rationale that differs from that assumed for other industries and sectors: this could be a major influence upon the depth and duration of a domestic recession. In addition to buoyant demand for plant and machinery in recovery and boom phases of an economic cycle, which could justify the release of catalytic events from the plant and machinery sector, there would also be the prospect of a major derived demand for new plant and machinery which reduced costs, improved quality, or altered prevailing economies of scale when firms in particular industries were being squeezed by depressed markets or new competitors. Catalytic events developed within the plant and machinery sector, which included any of the three features mentioned above, could be released or brought forward to capitalize upon the perceptions that the targeted industrial customers could not afford to delay purchase. The precise rationale of a possible strategy to accommodate the derived demand from depressed industries would be difficult to anticipate. Nevertheless, the probability is that there would be a critical period, before severe depression, during which there was an effective derived demand and beyond which firms could no longer afford to make the investment and collapse was inevitable.

A second influence, that would assume a more prominent position in an economy deficient in a plant and machinery sector, would arise from the unpredictable appearance of non-corporate, catalytic activity. Private individuals, and small groups of individuals, operating outside existing organizations are anticipated to realize entrepreneurial events to minimize costs, or rather to contain costs within highly inflexible budgets: it is assumed that they will not be able to afford to attempt to maximize their investments' yield by withholding its release until market demand is judged to be most favourable. Under such conditions, there would be a random pattern of very reduced catalytic activity even during recessionary and depression phases and there would be the subsequent effect on the potential for allocating activity.

The third and final influence would arise from the natural reinvestment or restocking effect which is identified in conventional trade cycle theory. In the absence of a catalytic entrepreneurial event the operation of the omega phase, which is by definition temporary, would eventually be followed with reinvestment and restocking by surviving firms, causing an increase in economic activity. It should be remembered that throughout this process the operation of the secondary wave would be expected to be affected. The combination of multiplier effects upon demand and accelerator effects upon investment, when overlaid with changing expectations of a more optimistic nature in recovery, and a more pessimistic nature in recession, would then further augment the upswings and downswings of this cyclical process.

CYCLICAL DISTURBANCES

The simple cyclical process described above would in practice be disturbed by a number of factors.

In the absence of exogenous shocks to the system, there is no reason to suppose that all firms will release catalytic entrepreneurial events *only* under conditions of rising economic activity. It can be argued that some firms would attempt to counteract the impact of recession by releasing previously withheld catalytic entrepreneurial events in an attempt to revive their trading conditions. An important caveat to the observation that this could, in itself, lead to a cyclical upturn due to the increased demand for plant and equipment which subsequent allocation events would imply is that these would need to refer to domestic producers. In the event that the production potential for such requirements resided in foreign economies, then the economic boost provided will also tend to occur in those economies and not in the domestic economy. This implies a key role for the producers of plant and equipment in facilitating economic resurgence within an economy. Those economies which lose the ability to respond internally via the production of investment goods to disseminate catalytic events will necessarily forego much of the development potential which could have resulted. Similarly, some firms will naturally release catalytic entrepreneurial events in a period of recession, where these refer to process innovations which reduce production costs. The demand for this kind of entrepreneurship will be considerable when firms which would benefit by its innovation are under pressure to reduce unit costs. The same points made above apply on the aggregate economic impact which would be expected.

A further source of disturbance to this cyclical phenomenon, which relies fundamentally on the propensity for most catalytic entrepreneurial events to be released during periods of increasing economic activity, arises from the operation of the individual catalyst. It has been argued that such individuals are least likely to succeed in the realization of entrepreneurial ideas. It has also been observed that individuals may prove exceptions to the rule. Where this is the case and where the event which they realize is more fundamental in nature, having potential application to a wide number of industrial sectors, then clearly the regular cyclical activity which the simple model would predict could be disturbed and distorted.

A further major and obvious source of disturbance in this cyclical process is represented by the incidence of exogenous shocks to economic activity. It is assumed that these are entirely unpredictable and are caused by non-economic factors. Examples would include the impact of a good or a bad harvest, the incidence of war, and acts of God. Clearly there are also many permutations in terms of events, which have both economic and non-economic elements. Examples of these would include the incidence of drought in some countries of the world which may distort market equilibrium in those countries, and also the reallocation of food reserves between countries.

The last source of major disturbance which is considered in this section on cycles in economic activity is perhaps one of the most interesting in that it refers to the recursive relationship between macroeconomic policy, macroeconomic events, and entrepreneurship.

THE MACROECONOMIC FEEDBACK CYCLE

The design of macroeconomic policy is a function of actual and anticipated macroeconomic events combined with the prevailing accepted or conventional 'economic' wisdom. Whatever the particular doctrine accepted, it is clear that since the impact of the Keynesian interventionist stance of the 1950s and 1960s in many developed economies, the role of the state in economic activity has become large. In this sense macroeconomic policy and macroeconomic intervention still occur even though traditional Keynesianism has been largely rejected.

Different academic and political positions lay emphasis on different control variables for the manipulation of macroeconomic events. Such control variables would include, for example, the level of the PSBR and government consumption, the rate of interest, and the exchange rate. It is not the purpose of this analysis to investigate the differential impact of these individual control variables or their relative frequency of usage under different economic attitudes and interpretations. The extent of any volatility or usage of such control variables however will naturally affect the levels of uncertainty confronting firms. The impact of this uncertainty upon the entrepreneurial venture at all levels will be determined primarily by the extent of that volatility, and therefore the greater caution which must be used in formulating projections and forecasts of firm's future costs and revenues. Clearly the greater the volatility and inconsistency in the application of significant control variables, the more serious the impact upon firms' ability to plan for the future.

Just as the control variables and major macro conditions which operate will influence entrepreneurial events at each level in terms of the categories used, so entrepreneurial events will influence macroeconomic conditions by their aggregate impact and therefore influence the macroeconomic policy decisions which are taken. The unpredictability which pervades the impact of changing macroeconomic conditions upon different types of entrepreneurship is also in operation in the reverse case. It is very difficult, if not impossible, to identify how changes in the incidence of different types of entrepreneurial event will influence the macroeconomic conditions which obtain and through them further influence the macroeconomic policies which themselves affect entrepreneurial events.

The influence of entrepreneurial events, and in particular catalytic entrepreneurial events, is probably more significant in terms of the rate of change of the secular trend, rather that the short- and medium-term fluctuations around it. Since economic development is a long-term consideration, then it is perhaps with this view in mind that the policy implications of the considerations raised can be discussed.

SUMMARY

In this section of the text we have attempted to clarify the economic contribution of entrepreneurship by viewing it in terms of the markets for factors of production. This extension of traditional analysis is designed to divert attention from the role of entrepreneurs as individuals towards the practical considerations of constraints upon the successful realization of events.

Having dispensed with the natural inability to predict the nature of future entrepreneurship we focus upon the conditions confronting the potential perpetrators.

Given the constraints upon the successful realization of entrepreneurial events, we have also considered a reinterpretation of the macroeconomic implications of their eventual impact and the recursive nature of that relationship. Our overriding objective, however, is to place these observations within a practical and relevant format in terms of policy design, since it was the upsurge in policy applications to encourage 'entrepreneurship' in many market economies, which provoked the preceding analysis. It is for this reason that the following section (Part Three) on policy options and information requirements is so necessary since it completes our coverage.

The bridging exercise between theoretical observation, practical consideration, and realistic policy options is naturally discomforting in terms of the style of approach. Having generated a series of arguments towards a clearer view of entrepreneurship, however, it is incumbent upon us to explain how these refer to practical policy design.

REFERENCES

1. Schumpeter, J. A., *The Theory of Economic Development*, Harvard University Press, Cambridge, Mass., 1934.
2. Schumpeter, J. A., *Business Cycles: A Theoretical Historical and Statistical Analysis of the Capitalist Process*, 1st edn, 2nd impression. McGraw Hill, Maidenhead, 1939.
3. Schumpeter, *Theory*, p. 225.
4. Ibid.
5. Ibid., p. 228.
6. Ibid., p. 241.
7. Ibid., p. 252.
8. Ibid., p. 91.
9. Ibid., p. 93.
10. Ibid., p. 232.
11. Ibid., p. 241.

POLICY AND INFORMATION

INTRODUCTION TO PART THREE

The realization of an entrepreneurial event requires the combination of human and financial capital. The entrepreneurial input is contained within the human capital but has very specific characteristics. The financial capital reflects a derived demand for the control of non-monetary or secondary inputs. The following three chapters consider the role for policy under the headings that were identified in Part Two where the focus was on factor market analysis. The first chapter in Part Three addresses policy for entrepreneurship, the next finance, and the third secondary inputs.

Previous chapters have considered definitions and theories of entrepreneurship, together with categories of entrepreneurial activity while acknowledging the dynamic nature of factor markets confronting entrepreneurs. It is clear that no simple recipe of policy prescriptions is likely to be adequate. Policies designed to impinge upon entrepreneurial activity require clear specifications in terms of the entrepreneurial contribution required and the time horizons for impact. Certain types of entrepreneurial activity have been identified that, if successfully stimulated by general policies, may not be capable of affecting economic development and may even promote outcomes that are unwanted by policy makers such as a proliferation of new firms in declining industrial sectors, for example.

The design of policy initiatives requires a clear identification of objectives and an appreciation of the economic mechanisms through which the objectives might be achieved.

Broad aims for policy initiatives are relatively easy to generate and typically refer to economic growth and full employment of the labour force. From an operational perspective, these aims provide little indication of a structured or relevant approach: they never identify the mechanism by which the outcomes are to be achieved. It is necessary to assume that all entrepreneurial activity is desirable and that policy initiatives should focus on those most apparent constraints thought to restrict entrepreneurship. In such circumstances the nature and volume of unrealized entrepreneurial activity becomes highly significant for the policies to be successful. While it is clear that inventiveness and entrepreneurial activity are not synonymous, unrealized activity could imply inventions and new ideas that are not innovated because of factor market constraints. Alternatively, unrealized activity could reflect ideas that are not viable and that it is not efficient to pursue from either a business or economic perspective.

As the preceding analysis has demonstrated, the concepts of development and factor markets are dynamic. Policy is concerned with the course of economic change. It is unlikely that the objectives can refer to the achievement of a specified set of conditions but rather to the direction and speed of change. Similarly, if it is accepted that different conditions imply different policy prescriptions, then policies should be dynamic and fluid, reflecting the changes that are taking place. In terms of the development process, policy can be used to effectively negotiate constraints that are considered undesirable but it cannot stimulate prespecified entrepreneurial events.

Policy design must refer primarily to factor markets and the constraints that prohibit them working efficiently. It is irrational to pursue particular patterns of economic change and particular resource allocations in the medium to long term that maximize the output of economic activity because future patterns of demand and supply are unknown. While the explicit objective of maximization is inappropriate for political and social reasons, the principle of the argument holds. The development process will include entrepreneurial events which no direct policy intervention could plan to achieve.

Policy initiatives may offer certain rewards in terms of potential development but they also involve risks. Evaluation of this risk reward balance must be speculative. In the case of catalytic and allocating events the particular outcome is unknown by definition. The major problem is that of relevant information and its adjunct, imperfect foresight. The nature of requisite information will change and combined with the Austrian-type spectre of perpetual disequilibrium, the policy designer is faced with a daunting task. Simplifying assumptions which allow a comparative statics approach are also very limited because the adjustment process of principle concern to the policy designer is completely ignored.

The above is not presented as an excuse to avoid more rational and structured approaches to policy: when constraints can be anticipated from a theoretical perspective the problem resolves to one of correct empirical identification. It must also be acknowledged, however, that effective constraints are not necessarily of a purely economic character. Natural constraints could describe imperfections such as externalities in the market process. In the absence of policy intervention an unfettered allocation of resources is considered undesirable. Unnatural constraints could then refer to situations where the political and social systems impinge on the economic system with unwanted economic consequences. It is probable that both categories of constraint would interest policy-makers but in the case of unnatural constraints there are necessarily trade-offs beyond the prerogative of an economic treatment.

The purpose of the following three chapters is to examine broad responses to general imperfections and constraints that impinge upon entrepreneurial activity at a national or regional level. Particular policies or approaches are cited as illustrative examples or options: no attempt is made to specify a restrictive set of assumptions that would be required to provide the detail of any policy. The approach taken in this section tries to accommodate the strategic focus adopted when referring to entrepreneurship and the more orthodox, tactical focus when referring to finance and secondary inputs.

NINE

POLICY FOR ENTREPRENEURSHIP

INTRODUCTION

The preceding chapters have attempted to isolate elements of the role played by entrepreneurship within a dynamic economy. The theory of entrepreneurship developed here, if accepted, naturally facilitates an approach to policy that differs fundamentally from the approaches adopted by policy-makers in the past. In particular, a policy framework can be developed that has a strategic perspective as well as a tactical component. Furthermore, there is the possibility of engaging tactics to suit specific, economic conditions that while consistent with an overall strategy, accommodate the dynamic character of any regional or national economy.

It has already been stressed that the success of policy can only be gauged if the purpose or objectives of the policy have been made explicit. The assumption taken here is that entrepreneurship contributes primarily to economic development: there may, or may not be a relationship between economic growth and employment generation. Here it is argued that it is inappropriate to look to entrepreneurship to create employment whereas it is completely appropriate to look to entrepreneurship to facilitate economic development. The mission of the policy-makers for which our discussion would be most apposite takes the following form:

> to achieve that rate of economic development considered desirable and worthwhile within the social and political confines of a particular economy, be that local, regional or national.

This choice of mission, from which more specific and quantifiable objectives could be drawn, explains in part the lack of coincidence between policy rationale put forward here and policy prescriptions employed in practice. Furthermore, entrepreneurship cannot be equated with starting or running a new business. It is only when there has been an unrehearsed combination of resources motivated by the uncertain prospect of temporary monopoly profit that there is evidence of entrepreneurial activity. Replicating existing business forms and activities will have a largely negative impact unless there are clear profit signals to do so.

Even within the more restricted definition of entrepreneurship used here there remain classes of entrepreneurial activity that may have unwanted affects on regional or national economies. Simultaneously there are other classes of entrepreneurship that are particularly required at key points in the cyclical development of an economy.

Corporate entrepreneurship will be a major component of any aggregate volume of entrepreneurial activity and it is odd that policies to date have tended to focus principally upon individuals and new businesses with a lesser, or secondary focus, on small groups and existing businesses; there has been no policy directed at corporate entrepreneurship.

Finally it has been a central strand to the arguments developed in this text that the economy is dynamic and that any prescribed tactics must change to follow a consistent strategy. It is for this reason that the discussion presented does not concentrate on the minutiae of possible schemes but rather focuses on the broader rationale of particular tactics.

PRIMARY CONSIDERATIONS

Policies addressing the supply of entrepreneurship or entrepreneurial activity have qualitative and quantitative aspects. It has been argued that the absolute number of aspiring entrepreneurs may not be as significant as the complement of key categories of entrepreneur. Given a particular mix of entrepreneurial types, however, the absolute number may still be important. The quality of aspiring entrepreneurs, as inferred from the proportion of viable entrepreneurial events orchestrated, is absolutely critical. The options available to policy designers who attempt to influence the quality, quantity, and mix of entrepreneurs directly are essentially long-term and speculative. For this reason the level of commitment for such policies is difficult to calculate. The level of return cannot be hinted at prior to the investment, and subsequent evaluation would be difficult or impossible to quantify after the event.

These problems are not unique to entrepreneurship and working political solutions have traditionally been found for similar problems. The nature of policy options that relate solely and explicitly to the entrepreneurial function, rather than to the associated aspects of the entrepreneurial activity, can be usefully approached in an elemental way and according to that part of the mechanism that is suspect or deficient.

The mechanism, or entrepreneurial system, that is being accepted here has three basic components or subsystems. Each of the subsystems is seen to fulfil a particular function; these are summarized below:

1. a continual generation of development potential through the materialization of catalytic entrepreneurial events;
2. the efficient exploitation of that potential through the materialization of allocating entrepreneurial events;
3. the efficient realignment and operation of affected industries and organizations through refining entrepreneurial events.

Constraints or impediments on any one of these subsystems will have negative implications for economic development. Entrepreneurial activity within these three spheres will be induced or suppressed by different factors and policies. Most critical for the longer term development of an economy will be the catalytic activity: in the medium term, development will be achieved through the allocating activity. Without there being a flow of catalytic events, however, the allocating activity will become less productive and add less value as diminishing marginal returns set in, reflecting a fixed stock of development potential. Refining activity is essentially a short or immediate-term response and does not contribute to development directly although it does have implications for the effectiveness of efficient allocations.

From a policy perspective there is the potential to facilitate or impede the operation of the system as a whole. Additionally there is the potential to facilitate or impede the subsystems individually. Within the subsystems, entrepreneurial activity can be instigated by the corporate and non-corporate entrepreneur. Policies can be designed that develop one source of entrepreneurship over and above the other. When considering the tactics of a strategic policy that is required to affect the level and success of entrepreneurial activity therefore, it is useful to explicitly consider the tactics as they apply to:

1. (a) catalytic corporate entrepreneurship;
   (b) catalytic non-corporate entrepreneurship;
2. (a) allocating corporate entrepreneurship;
   (b) allocating non-corporate entrepreneurship;
3. (a) refining corporate entrepreneurship;
   (b) refining non-corporate entrepreneurship

Here it is assumed more likely that policy-makers will be concerned to increase the aggregate level of viable entrepreneurial activity rather than decrease it and so our attention is restricted to policy designed with the intention of increasing the supply of entrepreneurs pursuing viable events. Some of the policy tactics will be particular to the individual subsystems and the components of those subsystems; at an initial, more fundamental level, however, there will be tactics that are not so specific.

The human capital that entrepreneurship presupposes can itself be divided into two categories. On the one hand there are attitudinal aspects of

entrepreneurship which evoke ideas of proactivity, creativity, and original-
ity, while on the other hand there will be technical or functional aspects of
entrepreneurship that evoke ideas of management, business, and commercial
skills. Attention to these areas at a pre-employment or entrepreneurial stage
would provide a foundation on which more immediate and direct policies
could be built.

CREATIVITY AND ENTREPRENEURSHIP

Entrepreneurship has been defined in terms of 'new or unrehearsed combinations' of economic resources. By this definition it is implied that some
product, process, service, or system is created that previously had not existed.
For this activity to be converted from a conceptual to a practical application
with economic significance requires a combination of problem-solving and
ingenuity together with a motivation. The motivation has been assumed to
arise from 'the uncertain prospect of monopoly profit'. This potential profit
can finance independence or security or any of the other more overtly
psychological motivations. The scope for policy then focuses on the elements
of creativity, problem-solving, and the level of profit. Policy addressing
effective retained profits for the individual or individuals concerned, as well
as for the company or corporation specifically, are readily transparent and
will not be pursued here.

The education system is the immediate mechanism through which the twin
aspects of creativity and problem-solving can be approached. The pedagogic
rationale for approaches to education, however, shifts in much the same way
as economic rationale shifts. In terms of creativity there could be merit in a
shift of emphasis from the traditional teaching by explanation and demon-
stration towards approaches that rely on discovery and hypothesis building.
The practical and idealized solutions, however, are unlikely to have much in
common when budget and resource constraints generally dictate the best that
can be achieved. It is anticipated that any movement from the status quo
would involve increased expenditure, at least in the short term, and contextual inertia as discussed in previous chapters that would exacerbate genuine
budgetary difficulties. The investment necessary would generate very
uncertain returns that would be difficult to isolate from other influences in
anything other than the very long term.

Giving pupils and students access to information and opportunity to
process that information in constructive and relevant ways requires
additional information or different skills to those required in conventional
classroom situations. The size of pupil groups that can be processed
realistically will also differ from common classroom sizes. Economies of scale
and measures designed to raise the apparent cost-effectiveness of teaching
staff are unlikely to engender the attitudinal characteristics associated with
entrepreneurship. Similarly it is unlikely that teaching staff with limited

horizons and an unawareness or hostility to a broader commercial and industrial world will create an atmosphere conducive to the development of creativity in the sense it is used here. Policy designers in any one economy can monitor educational innovations and investment levels occurring in other economies and stimulate the research necessary to formulate coherent policies. It has to be accepted that the role of competing approaches to the provision of education in the determination of attitudinal qualities is little understood.

BUSINESS SKILLS AND ENTREPRENEURSHIP

Within the last decade the requirement for basic business skills has been recognized in the UK, for example, following the commitment to stimulate the 'enterprise culture'. Management education has been available on a very limited scale for much longer and received major impetus in the 1960s and the late 1970s. Professional training in functional business disciplines, particularly accountancy and business law, has a longer history. It is striking to note that functional specialisms have justified education and training whereas general business skills for entrepreneurship have not. Throughout the 1980s in the UK and elsewhere there has been a proliferation of courses and programmes aimed at those adults who have expressed a clear intention to start a new business of one kind or another. Simultaneously, there has emerged a corporate interest in intrapreneurship, new venturing, management of change, and other 'buzz-titled' programmes essentially aimed at equipping employees with the skills to become entrepreneurs.

For those individuals not entering further education or managerial positions in large companies, the opportunity for business training is nearly non-existent. During that part of the compulsory, educational process there is little focus on business skills although there is an immediate suitability for an application in more formal and established subjects. Perhaps it is an indictment of the perceived role of entrepreneurship that it should be undertaken only when the prospect of success is minimized. In view of the significance of the financiers' assessment of the promoter in any application that an entrepreneur makes for funds, and external equity in particular, it could be anticipated that financial constraints will be often cited as a major obstacle in the formation of a new enterprise. The non-investment of funds in a new enterprise on the grounds of the promoter's naivety becomes a self-fulfilling prophecy in so far as the business can not succeed without funding. Nevertheless, the financier's assessment is unlikely to be favourable if training and general awareness of business skills are so difficult to acquire. A further feature of this bizarre curricular omission is the modern response it has generated. In relation to the education and training considered necessary to equip an individual to become an accountant, doctor, engineer, or even a manager, those courses and programmes now available to aspiring or committed founders of new business are inexplicable: there are no courses in the UK, for example, that provide more than four weeks' formal input.

The attitudinal and functional elements of entrepreneurial activity briefly referred to above are seen as obvious facilitators for any ensuing entrepreneurial behaviour and are anticipated to impinge positively on the potential stock and quality of entrepreneurs within an economy.

The impact of an educational orientation of the type suggested could have additional benefits, that in themselves justify greater commitment to the approach. For students and pupils with no sympathy or inclination to be entrepreneurs themselves, an appreciation of the purpose and contribution required within a commercial environment and an awareness of the mechanics by which an effective contribution generates income and profit, would facilitate communication and efficiency within organizations. Simultaneously, an awareness of skills and techniques that can be employed usefully to assess or manage any type of venture operating within resource constraints could in part dismantle the resistance to business and management training at subsequent stages in an individuals' career.

Within many countries the accepted approach to acquiring business and entrepreneurial skills has been experiential; the emphasis being upon 'learning by doing' and 'learning from mistakes'. This is obviously a costly and inefficient process for a manager or director within an existing organization and a critical process when undertaken in a new or small business. The high disappearance and failure rates of new and small businesses in particular is not necesssarily an inescapable fact of life but one that reflects a naïvety and ignorance that is consistent with inadequate and restricted access to relevant training and education. It is widely accepted that the failure rate, in terms of human mortality, is reduced by a high level of training and education for surgeons: there is clearly an analogy to be drawn between surgeons, entrepreneurs, and even business managers.

For an economy at any one point in time, however, the stock of potential entrepreneurs has to be taken as given. It may be that an inadequate level of apparent entrepreneurial activity is taken to indicate that the given stock is too small but, equally, the situation would be consistent with an adequately large stock that is restricted in one way or another from pursuing potential entrepreneurial events. Clearly, policy aimed at increasing the future stock of potential and actual entrepreneurs will be demonstrably ineffective if their activity is prohibited by other factors. In much the same way, policy designed to remove constraints on entrepreneurial activity will be unsuccessful if there is not an effective stock of aspiring entrepreneurs.

A major element in effective policy design will be an accurate diagnosis of the economic condition: reliable and relevant information is crucial and is discussed in greater detail in a subsequent chapter. It is only with an appropriate level of empirical detail, however, that the effective response of policy can be determined. The remainder of this chapter assumes that this major constraint to policy formulation can be overcome.

POLICY FOR CATALYTIC AND ALLOCATING ENTREPRENEURSHIP

It is accepted here that the quality, quantity, and mix of catalytic and allocating entrepreneurship is the most crucial aspect of the development process. Catalytic entrepreneurial events may represent a small proportion of the total entrepreneurial events being enacted within an economy. The impact of these events, however, has a disproportionate impact upon an economy if supported by allocating events. The catalytic event represents the only endogenous shock to an economic system from which development can ensue. Much of the previous discussion has emphasized the improbability of the private individual, or small groups of individuals, enacting a catalytic event. It was considered more probable that catalytic events would tend to be efficiently and successfully pursued by corporate entrepreneurs working within, and supported by, an existing organization. It was also noted however, that strategic considerations of the host organization may dictate the release of catalytic events in a way that exacerbates any cyclical tendencies within an industry or economy. The exception to this would be the possibility of counter-cyclical effects from corporate entrepreneurs operating within that sector which supplies plant and equipment to other industries and sectors. It is anticipated that there could be strategic advantage in particular circumstances from launching innovatory plant and equipment when the targeted customers cannot afford to delay the investment. During recessionary conditions in particular, policy specifically aimed at corporate entrepreneurs operating in a plant, machinery, and equipment sector will have the most immediate prospect of success.

Where policy has an urgent purpose to avert depression, or stimulate recovery, it is inappropriate to pursue initiatives other than than those which bring forward strategically withheld events. The gestation period from conception to commercial launch of an entrepreneurial event is influenced by a combination of many factors that can not be simultaneously addressed by policy. Whereas there may be initiatives that work in the right direction they can not be described as successful if they fail to achieve their objective within the given time horizon.

To induce a larger, more even stream of catalytic events generally, however, rather than simply bringing forward events that would occur anyway, requires there to be additional incentive to invest in the incubation of such projects and that strategic considerations which determine the appearance of events are reduced. For the corporate entrepreneur tax reliefs or credits could be the most obvious and powerful incentive. The precise operation of such a scheme would reflect the conditions within a particular economy and the commitment of the political decision-makers. Tax reliefs may apply only in one accounting period, or cover the first 5, 10, or 20 years of the operation. The relief may be partial or total, removing altogether the company's tax liability on entrepreneurial profit. Similarly, the relief may apply only to that surplus attributed to the entrepreneurial activity or it may apply to the organization's entire trading surplus. Taxing entrepreneurial profit at the company level and at the personal level is deficient in rationale except for the immediate contribution to public coffers. If the orthodox regime of double taxation inhibits entrepreneurial activity of a catalytic type, the negative implications for the ensuing allocating and refining activity would be significant. The impact on growth could imply that the opportunity cost of double taxation is too high and that such a regime is indeed myopic. For bureaucratic and fiscal purposes the entrepreneurial profit could be linked to products or processes centrally registered. The mechanism could be much the same as that currently used to safeguard the commercial rights to technical innovations and inventions.

For the non-corporate entrepreneur the prospect of tax relief might be perceived as an additional reward for the endeavour rather than as an inducement to initiate the enterprise; if this were to be the case the impact of tax reliefs may be insignificant. More influential for the non-corporate entrepreneur would be policies that reduce the opportunity cost of foregoing salaried employment to pursue the pretrading research and development phases and the pre-profit, establishment phase. The Enterprise Allowance Scheme in the UK, for example, is one scheme that has this affect although the scheme is not focused on entrepreneurial activity and embraces any individual who pursues a new business. Catalytic events, it has been argued, are typically the most difficult, time-consuming and expensive to orchestrate. The human capital of the successful instigator will be high. For an intitiative such as an enterprise allowance scheme to facilitate non-corporate catalytic activity where that activity would not have occurred otherwise requires the time horizon and value of any payments to be set at an effective level: the significance of such a scheme will reflect political judgement but it is important to differentiate between compensation and inducement. It is accepted that the Enterprise Allowance Scheme as it is operated in the UK is primarily concerned with encouraging self-employment among that part of the labour force which is unemployed and which has a low, or zero, opportunity cost; its purpose is not to induce entrepreneurship in the sense that is accepted here although there may be entrepreneurs who are marginally better off than they would be without the scheme.

In view of the economic significance of catalytic events and their role as a source for subsequent allocating opportunities, there could be major advantage in concentrating policy on this type of entrepreneurial activity. The cost-effectiveness of targeting corporate and non-corporate catalytic activity could be very much greater than blunderbuss policies aimed at increasing the number of new business registrations. Furthermore, in recessionary conditions when the contribution of catalytic and allocating entrepreneurial events is required and pursued most urgently, it can be anticipated that the significance of omega entrepreneurs and 'me-too', 'new to business persons' will be higher than at other times with possible unwanted economic implications. There will be social and political reasons for encouraging the temporary employment that these activities generate but they do not necessarily and automatically compensate for the negative economic implications of displacement.

The new knowledge or lateral thought embodied in a catalytic or allocating event only needs to be encouraged if it can be shown to be a constraint upon the development of these events. A more probable constraint would emerge from there being ineffective channels for potentially viable concepts to be adopted by effective entrepreneurial teams.

Organizational structures within trading businesses are not generally established to capitalize on entrepreneurship, rather they have evolved to manage that pattern of business that provides the raison d'être for the organization. An organizational structure that facilitates entrepreneurship is more likely to have a 'change orientation' as advocated by P. F. Drucker rather than the more traditional 'control orientation'. Managements and shareholders of existing companies may need to be educated and encouraged before basic and accepted business philosophies can themselves change. Greater and more frequent access to management education is an obvious route to facilitate the acceptance of corporate entrepreneurship.

From the perspective of the non-corporate entrepreneur there is the prospect of a constraint emerging from the lack of a mechanism to combine the twin inputs of conceptualization and orchestration. There will be individuals who generate or conceive new ideas with potential commercial application but also recognize they possess neither the expertise nor the enthusiasm to effectively pursue the concept. Similarly, there will be other individuals, or companies, for whom the acumen and resources are not obstacles but for whom the instigating concept is proving elusive or illusory. Attempts to establish 'ideas banks' and profile for 'inventors' through national, sponsored competitions have generally failed to grasp the very real issue of how any income streams generated can be distributed among the parties concerned and how the benefits of 'bought in', entrepreneurial concepts can be effectively sold to potential host companies.

Manipulating corporate tax rates to induce and reward entrepreneurial activity within existing corporations could be expected to affect the economics of acquiring or investing in, external entrepreneurial ventures and simultaneously raise interest in embryonic projects. In particular, policy initiatives that introduce the prospect of reducing tax liability on existing trading activities, in addition to any audited entrepreneurial surpluses, would substantially increase the effective demand of externally generated entrepreneurial events and concepts and raise the value of new companies attempting to orchestrate a catalytic event. Subject to the level of derived demand engineered by the taxation changes, and in addition to the extra corporate activity induced, there could become the prospect of an industry that specializes in the assembly and preparation of catalytic concepts or the development of new businesses pursuing particular entrepreneurial events with the explicit purpose of 'selling-on' to existing corporate customers.

Without there being a commercial rationale and effective market for potential catalytic and allocating events at the various stages of development, it is reasonable to expect that much of the potential for successful activity will be lost to any domestic economy and that the potential for, and realization of, economic development will be very much less than otherwise. In view of the synergy between catalytic and allocating events there may be little merit in distinguishing between categories for the implementation of policy. If fiscal relief was introduced then the prices that would emerge in an unfettered market for potential and actual events would work to achieve a balance between catalytic and allocating activity that could not be improved upon by policy. It would only be in the case of there being imperfections that resulted in a relative shortage of one of the categories of event that policy which differentiated between the events would be potentially useful.

The rate of uptake, refinement, and adaptation of registered catalytic and allocating events would also be increased throughout the economy as a whole by rejecting the current practice of securing entrepreneurial profit through registered patents and other restrictive mechanisms. Instead, interested parties could immediately start replicating and refining the product, process or system, without infringing any legal rights. In the absence of there being extra-entrepreneurial input, however, registration of something new would not be warranted and, while the tax advantages of the originator would be unaffected, there would not be tax relief for the replicator.

POLICY FOR REFINING AND OMEGA ENTREPRENEURSHIP

Omega entrepreneurship was excluded from the mechanism accepted to promote economic development. Policies to promote omega events are unnecessary and unwanted in the scheme of things accepted here. There may, however, be a case for introducing policy initiatives that inhibit omega activity in recessionary periods. The significance and negative impact of omega activity is very difficult to establish on *a priori* grounds and it could be, in any given situation, unnecessary to commit resources to formulating policy with the single purpose of restricting this type of activity. Where there are clear aberrations or imperfections, in markets or procedures that facilitate omega events, then there would be benefit from appropriate initiatives if social and political implications did not take precedence.

Refining entrepreneurship is anticipated to be useful for the efficiency of economic development but this type of entrepreneurial activity is largely reactive in nature and with marginal impact. Policy directed explicitly at inducing refining events would be of secondary importance to that policy aimed at inducing and facilitating catalytic and allocating events. The success of policy, and associated initiatives, with respect to catalytic and allocating activity would indirectly influence the requirement for effective refining activity by disturbing any approximation to a circular flow or equilibrium. As with policy for omega activity, policy for refining activity is more likely to be couched in terms of the removal of market aberrations and imperfections rather than in terms of positive discrimination. The difference however would be that the abberrations and imperfections targeted would be those identified as restricting refining activity rather than those which promote omega activity. The most obvious area for consideration is in those mature industries where extra profit or survival would ordinarily be dependent upon refining activity. It is in these industries and sectors that there has been the time and opportunity to become intimately aware of competitors' practices and to collude as loose but cosy cartels which can maintain profit levels without having to promote new entrepreneurial activities.

CONCLUSION

This brief treatment of policy for entrepreneurship has restricted itself to the underlying framework within which the detail of specific initiatives must fit. A particular economy, at a particular point in time, will dictate where the emphasis of policy should fall. The principal purpose of the discussion has been to keep separate and distinct those components which must be specifically accommodated in any coherent strategy.

The quality of entrepreneurial activity can be approached through education and training. The attitudinal implications however, determined by different approaches to education and training more generally may be crucially significant in ensuring that any specific input is worth while. Accommodating entrepreneurial and business orientated subjects within the school or college curriculum raises only administrative and political difficulties: at later stages in an employee's or employer's career there may be more substantial problems to overcome—not least in the allocation of costs incurred.

Our discussion of policy for entrepreneurship has distinguished between corporate and non-corporate entrepreneurs but there could be substantial merit in further dividing the categories. Corporations in particular, within which the corporate entrepreneurs are envisaged to operate, have connotations of size and maturity that could be taken to exclude most private limited companies. It is not accepted or inferred that these companies should be excluded from initiatives conceived to foster entrepreneurial behaviour.

On the contrary, it might be among the smaller, privately owned companies that policy would be most fruitful. It is these companies that are promoted on the grounds of their flexibility and responsiveness to customer requirements. Organizational structures and systems are not so formalized and the board of directors is not usually constrained by unknown shareholders.

Management buy-outs and spates of acquisitions are both phenomena that have gained prominence relatively recently. They have tended to be prompted by considerations other than the impact on entrepreneurial behaviour. Nevertheless, the potential significance of these trends could be substantial; the onus is with the policy-maker and political decision-maker to be sensitive to these and related developments and to exploit any opportunities for effective policy as they arise. In this sense, the institutions and accepted procedures for design and implementation of policy may themselves benefit from a more entrepreneurial flavour. Inertia and resistance to change, wherever it is found, represents an obstacle to entrepreneurship and a brake to development.

Finally it can be re-emphasized that apparent entrepreneurial activity can be confused with effective activity from a political perspective. Successful policy will only be characterized by potentially viable events. It might be that a reduced level of entrepreneurial activity that is characterized by lower failure rates and more spectacular successes would indirectly dismantle more psychological barriers and resistance to successful entrepreneurship than anything else.

TEN
POLICY AND FINANCE

For any entrepreneurial event to be realized there will be some minimum investment of finance. It may be that the funds required are very modest and that the entrepreneur chooses to ignore the monetary cost of the time invested but nevertheless there will be a requirement for funds. For the more ambitious projects the sums involved may be substantial and there may be significant time-lags before any return can be anticipated. If, for whatever reason, finance is not available, or is only available to a limited extent, then either entrepreneurial events will not be pursued by their originators or the event will be pursued with less than the minimum finance considered prudent, and the risk of failure will rise. Imperfections in the finance markets that constrain the flow of funds to entrepreneurial activity may be self-sustaining if there is a subjective over-assessment of the risk of failure, for example. In such a case, inadequate sums are made available and the number of undercapitalized operations will increase, as will the proportion that fail.

The initial sums required to finance the pre-establishment and pre-expansionary phases of entrepreneurial activity will ordinarily be small in a corporate context although large in a personal context. This situation is exacerbated when it is combined with the cessation of a reliable salary from a secure employer. Although there are financial instruments and procedures explicitly catering for entrepreneurial activity, these are relatively new and few in number. For the corporate entrepreneur the problems of generating the necessary finance can be very much easier, subject to the trading record of the employing organization and the shape of its balance sheet. It is on the non-corporate entrepreneur that the discussion here is focused. If the individuals concerned do not have access to personal wealth, then external supplies of finance become critical. Furthermore, it is ordinarily the case that an individual's holding of non-money assets greatly exceeds any holding of liquidity: if the mechanism for converting wealth into liquidity is faulty, then the individual could be constrained by a lack of finance.

Much of the discussion presented here necessarily covers aspects of an evolutionary process that is only complete when a new venture is generating its own positive cash flow. It is not possible clearly to differentiate the entrepreneurial process from the establishment and management of new and small firms in general. The point at which a successfully realized entrepreneurial event becomes the 'ordinary business' of running a firm cannot be precisely specified and, as such, much of the coverage presented here applies equally to new and small firm formation as it does to the realization of entrepreneurship *per se*.

The heterogeneity and untried aspects of genuinely entrepreneurial proposals provide potential financiers with a situation that they have not previously backed. Any decision to invest will carry with it a requirement to assess the entrepreneur's claims, and to take a level of risk that could be avoided or reduced in a portfolio of more orthodox investments. This, combined with the sums of money required, explain either exceptionally high returns or levels of security, required by external financiers.

Finally, it has to be recognized that identifying constraints on the supply of finance to entrepreneurial activity is a prerequisite for the design and implementation of effective policy, but differentiating genuine imperfections in the finance markets from perceived imperfections and injustices is problematic. It is recognized that apparent shortages of finance for entrepreneurial activity can arise either because the supply is constrained, or because the demand is inflated, perhaps reflecting prices for factor inputs that are higher than can be justified by efficiently operating markets or alternatively indicating unrealistic assessments of the projects prior to presentation for funds. Following the approach taken in the discussion of factor market analysis, the possibilities for intervention will be considered under the headings of equity and debt finance.

CONSTRAINTS ON THE SUPPLY OF EQUITY FINANCE

Equity gaps have been considered a constraint to new and small firms for many years. The discussion and policies generated have focused upon supplies of external equity, that is, investments made by third parties in exchange for the prospect of participating in any future profits of the company receiving the finance. Little attention has been paid to the possibility of there being constraints upon the availability of internal equity. There are many reasons why this should be so, but if it is acknowledged that expenditure is incurred before a proposal can even be presented to an investor, the significance of internal equity becomes paramount. In Chapter 7 it was recognized that internal equity need not only be represented by paid-up ordinary shares, held by the founders. Internal equity represents all those funds invested by the founders in a new embryonic business, which will be lost if the venture is unsuccessful. As such, internal equity will be required, even before a potential business is incorporated.

THE INTERNAL EQUITY GAP

When an individual, or group of individuals, adopt or generate an entrepreneurial vision, they do not have a complete set of formal data to justify the idea, and by virtue of the fact that the business does not at this stage exist, they cannot provide a track record or evidence of asset backing. As individuals, they may, or may not, be in a position to generate personal loans, but that ability is in no way related to the intrinsic merit of the entrepreneurial vision. For the entrepreneurs to pursue their initial insight some expenditure will be incurred—it may be modest expenditure initially—that can be easily met from personal liquidity. But before there is any identifiable business, the requirement for funds will escalate. The liquid reserves and unsecured overdraft facility of any individual will be limited. The funds invested in furthering the entrepreneurial vision may be internal equity if it is fed through a private limited company, or it may be quasi equity, if it is informally spent on research and development. The significant feature of this pre-start-up condition is that only internal equity can be used to finance the initial phase, and whether the funds are generated with personal debt, or directly from liquid reserves, is irrelevant.

The initial phase of a new entrepreneurial venture is completely reliant on internal equity. The characteristics of any particular entrepreneurial vision determine a minimum expenditure, before the proposal may be realistically presented to a potential financier. This minimum may be greater, or less than, the liquid holding of the proposer. In the case where the minimum exceeds the liquid holdings, personal debt has to be secured for the venture to continue. Ordinarily, the illiquid assets of the entrepreneur will greatly exceed any liquid reserves, and the potential significance of personal debt as a source of internal equity becomes apparent. If, for any reasons, there are imperfections in the market for personal debt, then there will be imperfections in the access to internal equity, unless the entrepreneur is prepared to liquidate personal assets and forego the utility that could have been generated from them. Where any personal assets are largely represented by property, which is simultaneously a home, a grave reluctance to liquidate the asset could be anticipated, whether or not the entrepreneurial venture proves successful. There is a clear distinction to be drawn between offering property as collateral that is only liquidated upon default, and liquidating property for the opportunity to pursue a venture. Furthermore, if there are imperfections or anomalies in the distribution and valuation of personal assets, these will have implications for the availability of internal equity. Immediately, major problems can be expected to arise.

First, an individual's ability to generate personal debt will be determined by the value of personal assets held and on the lender's attitude to the assessed ability of the borrower to discharge interest and capital repayments. Lenders may take the view that security guarantees repayment in the last resort, but that the borrower should be able to demonstrate an ability to repay the loan, without liquidating the collateral. Where this view is held the entrepreneur, in the research and development phase of the project, will be unable to demonstrate that the project is viable. The very purpose of the personal debt is to invest in internal equity so that the exploration can continue. It will be the case in the research phases that there is no definite prospect of generating income, unless development can proceed on a part-time basis. Furthermore, should the research indicate that the venture is viable, it would be unusual if it could generate the cash flow to service any debt in the immediate term. Under such circumstances it is completely conceivable that an individual could not raise the net value of any assets held, after an allowance for liquidation expenses.

An upper limit to the value of personal debt that can be generated would be related to the market value of personal assets. It has to be assumed that the value of an individual's assets correspond with the individual's requirement for internal equity. If this assumption does not hold good in practice, there arises a distribution problem that is outside the realms of economics. Where there is not a direct relationship between the personal wealth of an individual and the internal equity requirements of the entrepreneurial vision, there is the prospect of entrepreneurial events being abandoned by virtue of the entrepreneur's relative poverty. A significant observation that follows is that younger individuals will have had less opportunity to save part of any income and, everything else being equal, will ordinarily tend to have built up smaller holdings of wealth. Furthermore, it must be acknowledged that regional traditions and patterns of behaviour may have implications for the access to internal equity. Discrepancies in patterns of house ownership and house values, for example, could explain in part regional variations in the quantity and quality of entrepreneurial activity.

It must be stressed that these considerations apply principally to the early stages of an entrepreneurial venture, that is, before the vision can be researched and presented to a standard that will attract a commercial financier. A constraint on the supply of finance in these developmental stages, however, could be as significant, or more so, than constraints on the commercial operation of a new venture. It is important to recognize that constraints on the availability of internal equity will prohibit the development of an entrepreneurial vision, and therefore be less apparent than constraints on a trading business that is unable to expand or survive due to a lack of finance. It could be for this reason that factors affecting internal equity have been largely ignored, to the possible detriment of realized entrepreneurial activity.

THE EXTERNAL EQUITY GAP

The grounds for anticipating an external equity gap have been considered in Chapter 7. A supplier of external equity is primarily concerned with the anticipated real return on any investment made. Gathering and evaluating the relevant information and subsequently monitoring or overseeing the investment's progress, represent costs to the investor that do not vary in strict proportion to the sum of funds to be invested. These costs can more usefully be considered as fixed costs and dictate a minimum investment, below which the effective cost of £1 invested becomes prohibitively expensive. This economic minimum becomes higher as the overheads of an investing organization increase and as the performance of the other investments decline. A problem for entrepreneurs establishing high-risk firms, therefore, could be to find sources of external equity, where the overheads of the investor are low. Whereas it is prudent to establish a new venture with the minimum investment necessary to provide demonstrable evidence that the concept can be viable, there is an additional consideration of retaining the initial funding required to a level that exceeds any generally held minimum set by the institutional investors. Individual investors, rather than managed funds or institutions, would be more appropriate sources of finance for smaller packages of external equity.

The supply threshold and required rates of return of venture and development capital remains high and while this is the case, there will be the possibility of unfulfilled demand and a constraint upon entrepreneurship. It is those entrepreneurs who anticipate, or have prudently engineered, the prospect of establishing firms within relatively modest budgets, who will be affected. The initial requirement for finance can not be assumed to be related to either the ultimate potential of the venture, or the competence of the proposer.

The demand for equity below any threshold may be distinguished from the need for equity in this range; the demand may be anticipated to be smaller than the need to the extent of an acknowledged resistance among individual entrepreneurs to solicit or accept external participation. The resistance reflects a preference to maintain full control of the new venture and a resentment of financiers gaining the opportunity to participate in the firm's profits.

POLICY OPTIONS AND EQUITY GAPS

Personal debt instruments

Internal equity gaps can reflect an entrepreneur's lack of liquidity, an inability to demonstrate a guaranteed income stream with which to service any personal debt, or the inability to provide collateral that is acceptable to a lending institution. The criteria adopted by lending institutions are geared to protect their investors while earning an adequate profit for the institutions themselves. However, if these practices simultaneously incorporate anomalies that could prejudice entrepreneurship, particularly among younger individuals who have not had an opportunity to generate collateral from long periods of paid employment, or among individuals who have not had the opportunity or tradition to invest in private property, then policy intervention might be warranted.

Unless it can be assumed that personal wealth is correlated to entrepreneurial ability and inclination, anomalies in the availability of personal debt will provide internal equity constraints for a substantial portion of any stock of potential entrepreneurs. In principle there could be scope for a new personal debt instrument that accommodates the fact that younger individuals will, everything else being equal, have longer income generating futures. Currently in the UK, for example, there is no mechanism for the prospect of a long-term income stream to be converted into present-day purchasing power, except in the case of private-property mortgages. In the case of an individual accepting an option to borrow money over a long term, say 20 or 25 years, against a personal liability, and investing the funds in the early phases of an entrepreneurial event, there would be one of two possible outcomes. Either the entrepreneurial venture would not be adequately profitable to pay the salaries necessary to discharge the personal debt of the entrepreneur or the venture would be adequately profitable. In the latter case there is clearly no problem but in the former case the failed entrepreneurial event could be abandoned and the personal liability carried over.

The outcome of the entrepreneurial venture would generally be clear within five years, and probably within a very much shorter period. The failed entrepreneur would retain an obligation to discharge the personal debt with income from conventional paid employment. It would be inappropriate for an instrument with this character to have an associated repayment schedule that involved payments from day one of the term; rather it would be better to build in a 2- or 3-year repayment holiday so that a 25 year loan could be discharged over 22 or 23 years. Clearly the sums available to the entrepreneur would be a function of the individual's assessed opportunity cost. As such, there would be an anomaly in so far as income will not be a perfect proxy for entrepreneurial ability. Nevertheless, it might be supposed that any correlation would be stronger than between entrepreneurial ability and wealth which forms the basis for current procedures. The precise detail of a debt instrument with key characteristics to achieve the declared objective would be complex but not impossible to arrange: it is noted that there are already examples of loans to finance investment in human capital that fulfil a similar function, although with much shorter time horizons than are envisaged for investments in entrepreneurial activity.

External equity gaps are explained in part by the overhead costs of institutional investors. The overheads cover investments that fail or turn bad as well as the more conventional running costs. If the performance of the institutions themselves could be improved, then the range of an equity gap could be reduced. In practice there is already a strong incentive for commercial institutions to perform as efficiently as possible and it is unlikely that formal policy could improve the situation. An alternative approach for policy-makers would be to focus on non-institutional investors. An immediate approach is to provide incentives for individual investors to buy the shares of private limited companies. The Business Expansion Scheme in the United Kingdom is one example of a policy with precisely this aim. An incentive to the investor is provided through income-tax relief on the sums invested: such approaches potentially act on the supply of smaller packages of equity. The impact of the approach is determined by the details of the scheme and the size of the effective, post-tax return, to the investor. The lower the rates of tax being avoided, the lower the impact upon the supply of equity.

The difficulty of liquidating any investment made and a lack of familiarity with investment behaviour of this type have both acted as major impediments to private investors in the UK. Situations in which these considerations would be less significant, where for example the investor had additional, non-pecuniary interests in the venture, are largely excluded in the Business Expansion Scheme by virtue of the exclusion of lineally related investors. The precise rationale for the exclusion is not explicit, although it is accepted that tax-incentive systems can stimulate abuse and generate distortions elsewhere in the market process. Relative taxation rates on capital gains as against income flows will also have major implications for the perceived desirability of private investments in equity. Where there is no easily accessible market for the shares of private limited companies, liquidating a capital gain could be difficult or impossible to achieve. If the benefits to investors apply to capital gains only, then the significance of a reliable exit route becomes paramount. Provisions that allow a company to buy its own shares can be helpful in this context, as can Over the Counter (OTC) and Unlisted Security Market (USM) type developments. More effective, however, in overcoming the shortfalls in the markets and the transaction costs in particular, would be to reduce the need for them by designing the tax advantage to fall on income streams generated by the investments. The merit of this approach would be that the full benefit of the incentive to invest in the first place, would not fall exclusively upon a relatively small number of the highest income earners paying the highest marginal income-tax rates. More importantly, a preference to liquidate a successful investment as a capital gain would be reduced or removed if it was tax efficient to take the returns generated in the form of unearned income. In addition to negotiating inadequate or costly stock markets, there would be a reduced focus on arbitrary time horizons and the requirement for rarely attained equivalent compound growth rates in the very early years of an investment.

It has been suggested that the equity gap in part reflects constraints upon the supply of small parcels of risk capital, but also that the demand is restricted by the conditions attached to such investments. Clearly it is the prerogative of the entrepreneur to resist equity investments for whatever reason. There is, however, the possibility of further prejudicing the effective demand for equity if the two generic sources of funds, that is debt and equity, are treated differently from a company's point of view. In the United Kingdom the cost of debt funding is a tax-deductible expense that can be combined with other accepted trading costs. The dividend payment to equity-holders, however, is excluded from such a favourable treatment and is effectively unsubsidized money. Everything else being equal, there is super-ficially a strong incentive to minimize the equity in a business and maximize the value of a tax shield generated with debt. Whether it is appropriate to remove this asymmetry by treating debt in the same way as equity, or vice versa, could usefully be considered. A tax treatment favouring debt funding, as in the UK for example, could be interpreted as a factor inflating the demand for debt, and everything else being equal, would be one factor to explain rates of interest or collateral requirements being harsher than they would otherwise be.

More direct approaches to resolving equity gaps include 'marriage bureaux' operations that provide an interface for potential investors and investees. Alternatively, national investment banks can negate the need for private investors completely. The significant point, however, is that while imperfections remain in the supply of equity, it is impossible to judge the negative impact on the economy. The actual impact of those entrepreneurial ventures that are discarded will never be known. The corollary being that the cost-effectiveness of policies to remove any perceived, or actual, equity gaps can only be estimated after the event. The effect of an equity gap in practice is more likely to explain the high incidence of apparently undercapitalized firms, or firms with poor capital structures, rather than a complete dis-appearance of a big proportion of potential entrepreneurial ventures.

CONSTRAINTS ON THE SUPPLY OF DEBT FINANCE

The corporate debt market is concerned with the company's assets and the company's ability to service debt: recourse is not taken to the shareholders' personal assets in the case of default. In practice, at the modest levels of many new and small businesses in particular, the distinction between personal and corporate debt becomes unclear, with ostensibly business loans having the ultimate characteristic of personal debt; that is, the directors have personally guaranteed the debt or provided specific personal collateral. Nevertheless, if there are imperfections or anomalies in the corporate debt market there will be implications for new entrepreneurial ventures.

For new companies registered to provide the vehicle for the realization of an entrepreneurial event, there can be no track record of trading results which demonstrate an ability to service a loan. There are two immediate consequences from this: first, the significance of company assets becomes more crucial, and second, those assets are valued on a heavily discounted 'carcass' basis. Immediately a multiplier effect can be anticipated from imperfections in the equity markets discussed previously. In the absence of any debt funding, all assets held by a new company must have been financed by equity. If it is the case that there were to be no liquidation or administration costs, and the equity of the business had exclusively financed non-depreciating, readily saleable assets, then it might be possible to raise debt to a value that equalled that of initial equity, less servicing charges for the period of the loan. In these rather abstract conditions a deficiency in equity would restrict the debt available to a firm by a similar amount. In practice, the equity of a new business will ordinarily have financed expenditure on items and services that have no collateral value whatsoever and would be treated more like trading expenses than asset acquisition. Furthermore, those assets required by a new entrepreneurial venture, especially where the venture has many unique features and requirements, may not be readily saleable. There might not be any requirement for the bespoke plant and machinery made with just one particular and peculiar use in mind. The upshot of considerations of this kind is that pure, risk-free debt generated by a new company may be a small fraction of any equity invested, and it may be the case that a new company can not generate any debt within the first twelve months of trading. In these circumstances, and excluding the intrusion of personal debt, a new company would be disadvantaged to the extent of any tax shield associated with debt funding.

The problem of collateral provision and track record for new firms seeking debt is significant and reflects practices of lending institutions that have become established and accepted. This outcome of a market mechanism, however, can be negotiated by the implementation of policy if the anticipated benefits are thought to exceed the anticipated costs. Loan guarantee schemes are an example of policy designed to address the issue and have been operating in many countries for a number of years. Where schemes of this type are not available, the indigenous entrepreneurs are at a disadvantage. There are several important characteristics of a loan guarantee scheme that policy designers must consider. The operation of the scheme, for example, would refer to the mechanism through which the loans are allocated. In a large and complex economy it would be expensive to establish a distribution network. It could be argued that those institutions providing secured debt to established firms could operate the scheme and benefit from the guarantee in the event of default. In all respects other than the origin of the security, a new business could generate debt in the same way as an established business. The normal evaluation criteria applied by lending institutions are designed to maintain default rates within acceptable limits. If similar criteria are applied to loans under a loan guarantee scheme, the default rate would be expected to remain constant for this class of business. The interest rate charged by the lenders will reflect any marginal risk that they associate with particular customers. One potential danger of guaranteed loans operated by existing financial institutions, however, arises from the incentive to refinance existing, potential bad debts under the scheme. This could apply to loans which are unsecured because of the lender's initial, although misplaced, level of confidence with the borrower, but also to firms where there is a charge on directors' personal assets. The lender may prefer not to liquidate personal security because of the poor public relations it could cause. Short-term abuse of a loan guarantee scheme in this way could generate apparently high default rates in the early period of a scheme.

There are further implications deriving from the extent to which any loan is guaranteed. If the total loan is guaranteed there is a danger that the lenders' criteria may become less rigorous. At the margin, loans could be issued that would not be issued in the absence of 100 per cent guarantees. Default rates, again, might be expected to increase in these circumstances. An additional problem for the policy-maker refers to the cost of the debt to the borrower. If the objective of the scheme is to facilitate enterprise and entrepreneurship that is otherwise constrained by lack of track record, but more particularly by lack of collateral, it would be illogical to charge recipients a premium. Clearly those new enterprises relying on such a scheme would start trading with a cost disadvantage if the funds employed carried a substantial premium to cover the guarantee. Everything else being equal, default rates would increase with the operation of a premium. Perversely, if no premium was levied those enterprises generating debt in orthodox ways would, rightly or wrongly, perceive themselves disadvantaged if they had to jeopardize personal assets to secure loans. Manoeuvring might be anticipated so that more firms became apparently eligible for guaranteed loans and the demand under the scheme would greatly exceed initial expectations.

The aspects highlighted above indicate the possibility of high failure rates under a loan guarantee scheme or, alternatively, very substantial requirements for refinancing under the scheme by enterprises with conventional, secured loans. It could be argued that the absence of risk for those firms generating funds under the scheme would imply that their owner-managers would be less motivated to ensure the success of the project for which the funds were sought. This may or may not be the case; the principal difficulty with engineering a guaranteed loan scheme that is legally held by a new company, without at least one operational flaw, arises from its attempt to cater for equity shortages through a debt instrument. In restricted and particular applications a scheme could be useful but the limitations of the underlying concept would need to be accepted.

Loan guarantee schemes could be anticipated to have more successful applications in cases where the recipient firm is established, but the collateral value of its assets is very much lower than the book value. The very nature of some entrepreneurial ventures is such that uncommon raw materials may be required, for example, that are expensive to buy but almost unsaleable once delivered; manufacturing ventures with long production times can have substantial sums tied up in work in progress that is typically ascribed zero security value by institutional lenders; particular industries are characterized by slow payment for goods or services provided. In circumstances where these features apply, firms may be restricted from expanding or taking on extra orders because of the lenders' established criteria for valuing specific assets. A guaranteed loan scheme that catered for constraints upon expansion and establishment, rather than the initial start-up phases of a new venture, could be expected to have more controllable default rates.

FACTORS INFLATING THE DEMAND FOR FINANCE

The amount of finance necessary to pursue an entrepreneurial vision to the point where there is a viable business generating profits, at a given level of risk, is determined by the cost of factor inputs and established trading practices. Financial constraints on entrepreneurship could be interpreted as restrictions on the supply of either debt or equity, or as inflated demand. Earlier in this chapter it was noted that the favourable tax treatment of payments to debt holders, as against payments to shareholders, constituted one factor that would inflate the demand for debt and suppress the demand for equity. Everything else being equal, inflated demand for debt would ordinarily raise the rate of interest charged or the conditions attached to any borrowing. Thus there might be perceived to be a shortage of debt. In this section the intention is, very briefly, to consider one mechanism by which trading practices may inflate the requirement for finance.

DELAYED PAYMENTS

Small firms, and new firms in particular, that are establishing themselves in various markets for the first time, have to finance an initiation period that varies from industry to industry. Firms generating initial sales will experience pressure to supply their goods and services on terms that are consistent with the industry's norms. Furthermore, because of a lack of market strength usually associated with a new business entrant, potential commercial customers will be relatively strong and in a position to source particular products or services from a number of suppliers. With a new and vulnerable supplier, the commercial customer can gain better credit from the supplier by failing to discharge the invoice when it falls due. The new or small firm has no immediate recourse when this situation arises and is effectively at the mercy of the customer—subject to the usual practices of debtor management. There is clearly a delicate balance for the new firm to judge: too little pressure to secure payment for goods or services delivered is unlikely to be effective, while too much pressure could ensure that there are no repeat orders from potentially significant customers.

The problem of extended trade credit, that is credit taken over and above that stated in the terms of trade, became particularly acute when inflation and interest rates reached high levels in the 1970s. This economic period seemed to be habit-forming and delayed payment can still be a major determinant of a firm's requirement for funds to finance working capital. In most non-retailing operations the components of working capital, and thus the demand for finance, are related to the level of sales. The more successful a new operation becomes the greater the demand for working capital: everything else being equal, for a given level of sales the working capital requirement will increase with the amount of trade credit taken by a firm's customers. The value added in any viable operation ensures that cash outstanding from debtors will be a multiple of cash outstanding to creditors. The situation is further exacerbated because of the commercial insignificance of a new enterprise. An established supplier can often refuse to extend any credit to the new business and demand cash on delivery or pro forma invoicing. Where trade credit is awarded, the new business can not generally extend the credit period offered for fear of losing the supplier. New and small firms generally require more finance to cover this element of working capital than established and large firms. Why this situation exists is not completely clear. Legislation that addresses the problem could be straightforward and those businesses guilty of taking credit beyond that agreed to in a vendor's terms of trade could finance the mechanism to enforce the procedure.

The system of enforcement could be conducted through tribunals, industrial courts, or whatever, and it is quite possible that in many economies there might already exist a network through which the system could be operated. The disincentive from the knowledge that such a procedure is operational, combined with the deterrent of significant penalties levied against the offending firms, would benefit entrepreneurial activity by reducing the amount of finance required to launch a new business and, simultaneously, reduce the uncertainty in which businesses have to budget cash flows.

CONCLUDING REMARKS

In this chapter we have considered certain policy options and areas in which constraints may be alleviated or removed within the general categories of equity and debt finance. It is important to reiterate our initial observation, however, that there is a problem when attempting to distinguish between genuine market imperfections and those reported by firms which are a natural reflection of their particular trading conditions. We consider the question of equity constraints, both internal and external prior to an analysis of the policy issues which are raised. Our treatment of debt finance constraints and the possible application of loan guarantees is followed by a brief but important focus upon factors which inflate the demand for finance and the particular and often onerous problem of delayed payment.

A final and crucial observation is that intervention in the mechanisms which transmit finance to small business may be highly influential in their ability to expand or merely to survive, but carry the additional risk of supporting and extending the trading life of businesses which are marginal or suboptimal under existing commercial conditions.

ELEVEN
POLICY FOR SECONDARY INPUTS

As with the treatment provided in Part Two, the term 'secondary inputs' is taken to embrace all non-monetary inputs required during the realization of an entrepreneurial event. Three subgroups of secondary input are isolated for consideration here: they are plant and machinery, labour, and land and premises. These sections will be given relatively summary treatments since it is beyond the scope of this text to cover the very large areas of policy detail that can be applied. Distortions in the markets for these secondary inputs, which raise prices to levels higher than otherwise, will raise the amount of finance required to launch a new business, but secondly, they will adversely affect the trading costs of new operations. At the margin, new firms may appear unviable when faced with inflated input costs. It is also important to note that short-term policies covering labour and premises particularly are best designed in the local context, accommodating identified problems, whereas policies for entrepreneurship and finance can be considered from a national or regional perspective.

PLANT AND EQUIPMENT

For established and trading businesses there are two main areas in which policy designers have attempted to influence investment in plant and machinery. These refer to the use of purchase subsidies and depreciation allowances.

Subsidies can be a direct method of reducing the effective cost of plant and machinery and can be applicable to new entrepreneurial ventures as they are to existing businesses. Clearly subsidies introduced for items that are being traded in efficient markets will distort the allocation of resources and, everything else being equal, will increase the demand to levels that would not otherwise have been achieved. If the cost of subsidies is considered to be justified in terms of anticipated benefits, then the precise mechanism through which the subsidy is delivered will determine the usefulness for start-up businesses. Where the intention of a subsidy is to reduce the financial requirement of a venture, rather than promote the uptake of a particular technology for example, dispensing the subsidy upon demonstrable proof of purchase will not reduce the funds required. Applying a subsidy certificate to the purchase price of the asset, however, will reduce the funds required directly by the value of the subsidy. In the case of entrepreneurial events it is clearly impossible to predict the kind of investment purchases required and any subsidies would require to be non-product/service specific, subject to the purchase being represented as a fixed asset in the new company's balance sheet.

Selective subsidies have particular problems associated with them arising from the possibility of displacement which they risk. In these circumstances, firms which benefit from the subsidy have an artificial cost advantage which may manifest itself as price competition that cannot be matched by existing firms who are unaware of or unable to claim the subsidy. This can cause either a loss in profitability or a reduction in the output of existing suppliers and, at the limit, the closure of an unsubsidized but otherwise efficient competitor, i.e. displacement. This phenomenon makes the measurement of a subsidy's effectiveness extremely difficult. The relevant measure refers to additionality or the net change which has occurred. Where there are aspects of displacement evident it can be almost impossible to distinguish the impact of the subsidy from numerous other factors that impinge on the outcome.

In the case of the UK and the procedure which it adopts to collect VAT, for example, there is, in effect, a negative cash subsidy as opposed to a negative cost subsidy for new firms in the process of setting up. Most expenditure incurred is subject to VAT and is unlikely to be compensated from VAT levied on sales in the immediate term. The new firm is required to have greater access to liquidity than if the VAT mechanism operated in a different way. The VAT will effectively inflate the demand for finance among new firms where costs exceed sales and reduce the demand for finance among established viable firms where sales exceed costs.

Depreciation allowances are of more value to existing firms that are generating profits than they are to new ventures. In the first and second years of a new enterprise it is unlikely that profits will be generated against which to set depreciation. It is those businesses which anticipate a liability to corporation tax from a successful trading year that will be induced to invest more heavily as allowable depreciation rates increase.

LABOUR

The quantity, quality, and adaptability of the labour force, in particular regional skill patterns, and the ability to adapt to changing environments, are crucial for local economies. The prime focus of policy design, given the previous emphasis on the dynamics of the entrepreneurial contribution, is that of spatial and industrial mobility. Mismatches between the skills available and those required are almost unavoidable given the nature of economic change. At the same time these mismatches can constitute a considerable constraint to the dynamic process of economic development. There is clear merit in maintaining a flexibility within the labour force, so that changes in commercial and industrial requirements can be met without there being protracted periods of high unemployment.

As communication and information improve, so the lag between the appearance and refinements to catalytic events become less pronounced. The main determinant of the location of primary and, more particularly, secondary wave effects discussed earlier will be the flexibility of the labour supply. Where entrepreneurial events occur simultaneously in two different economies, the economy with more flexible labour supplies will experience fewer constraints, a shorter period of adjustment, and, everything else being equal, earlier innovation and wider, profitable dispersal of the adapted event throughout the industrial structure. It is often these secondary waves of innovation which lead to significant levels of investment and reallocation of factors of production. Countries which benefit from catalytic entrepreneurial events are not necessarily those in which the events initially occurred.

One of the major problems involved in implementing some form of training and education input to facilitate this desired flexibility is that of allocating a responsibility for the nature of the training and the investment in human capital which ensues. Co-ordination is important for the coherence of educational experience, but centralization may be inappropriate since regional and industrial variations imply different inputs and skill requirements. The danger of a regional focus is the possibility of reinforcing regional disparities if the training content reflects perceptions of 'new' industrial requirements in the absence of co-ordination with other regions where training patterns are also changing. In this situation regions may correctly identify a particular skill requirement for the near future and develop and provide training to the extent that, when taken in aggregate, there is an over-supply once the retraining is complete.

An alternative possibility may arise where there is competition between regions for the same skills. In this situation, training within relatively depressed areas may provide certain parts of the work force with the requisite skills to leave and obtain employment in more buoyant areas. This introduces the potential for a vicious circle, where attempts to regenerate industrially depressed areas via training only provide those who have been trained with the ability to command jobs in successful, rapid-development areas.

This implies a need for an integrated approach to training used in different regions and industries, and the matching of the training to the particular skill requirements of local firms. This level of co-ordination clearly requires a high degree of management. The problem here is that entrepreneurship, by its very nature, is very much a market-driven process. In the limiting case of catalytic entrepreneurship, the most appropriate training is by definition, unknown beforehand. These points imply the need for flexible training but perhaps, more particularly, they imply the importance of attitudinal and educational training, in conjunction with very limited and specific skills training. Attempts to reorientate orthodox education so that it has relevance to post-school employment and endeavour could be achieved by the broad approaches referred to in the discussion of policy for entrepreneurship.

There are two significant features of the labour market which impinge upon the financial requirements of entrepreneurial ventures and new businesses in general. First, if employees with the requisite skills are not readily available for the venture, the competition from existing employers will be strong and the relative cost of particular categories of labour will be higher than otherwise. Clearly firms, prior to their conception or incorporation, cannot assume the responsibility for training their own labour. The labour that is available will reflect public or private sector priorities that combine decisions and assessment from previous time periods. Second, training and the investment in human capital which it represents can be an expensive and unrewarding activity. The more successful and intense any training becomes, the more mobile and expensive the labour becomes. Whereas the mobility of labour is superficially a good thing within a domestic economy, if that mobility extends beyond the national boundary, the investment is lost and may even be detrimental, such as in the case of a 'brain drain'. Furthermore, if it is the businesses themselves that organize and fund training, only to lose trained employees before the investment in human capital has become economic, there will be no incentive for them to continue.

There is clearly an unresolvable time-lag between the requirement for particular skills and the availability of those skills if training is a market-driven process, and the possibility for inappropriate training if it is the outcome of more central planning mechanisms. At more sophisticated levels, where training is geared to refining and building upon existing skill and education patterns, the possibility for effective market-driven mechanisms becomes apparent subject to an efficient and competent market supply. Although individual firms may be able to purchase labour with the appropriate skills given sufficient finance, there is still a demonstrable need for policy initiatives at an aggregate, pre-employment level. Policy in a developed country can influence an economy's labour force in terms of the basic skill patterns, the flexibility of those skill patterns and the perceived desirability amongst potential employees towards subsequent privately financed training. It is beyond the scope of this discussion to consider the detail of basic education and training philosophies.

PREMISES

The major issues that relate to industrial or commercial premises can be classified as market and non-market features. Non-market features are typified by property taxes, such as local rates in the United Kingdom, and locational land-use restrictions reflecting planning procedures. Market features would be the derived demand for property and the time-lags required for the effective supply to satisfy demand.

Market conditions confronting firms vary through time, between regions and between industries. The ability of firms to meet property tax will similarly be reflected by the performance in any one trading year. Taxes that are based exclusively on occupied floor area, for example, will reduce the demand for space to levels smaller than otherwise but cannot accommodate the ability of firms to pay the tax in depressed conditions. There is clearly no merit in reducing the tax base by reducing the stock of trading businesses through the imposition of a tax that has been arbitrarily calculated. For new entrants to industrial and commercial premises, selecting occupants according to their anticipated ability to discharge property tax is a legitimate allocation process where the demand for space exceeds the supply. However, once installed and established, relocating is an expensive and time-consuming operation for commercial organizations. This consideration alone limits the usefulness of a rationing mechanism based on fixed tax rates.

Where there is a concern to promote the establishment of new businesses, as opposed to the maximization of the property-tax yield in any one time period, it is inconsistent to increase the finance requirements of the prospective business and, simultaneously, to effectively increase the trading costs of that new business. Corporation tax on a firm's profit accommodates the ability to discharge the tax but would not at the same time ration the consumption of floor space or accommodate externalities from different types of land use. Land-planning legislation and zoning, combined with the internalization of externalities, would directly accommodate specific environmental considerations. The efficient allocation of floor space is very much more problematic, however, due to the major costs of relocating.

The total land area available to any economy is, more or less, severely restricted and political trade-offs are required to distribute available and suitable areas to competing uses. The political process is beyond the scope of the treatment provided here. The price of land for particular uses, however, will be determined by the interaction of demand with this politically determined supply and hence the effective level of rents will be determined. At the margin, some firms will not be viable that would have been viable in the absence of planning regulations. Given a potential area for industrial and commercial use, any mechanism to allocate that area among competing uses would require a tariff or tax that is based on floor area. Property-tax rate bands that are a function of floor area and annual trading performance could provide the basis for a scheme to accommodate allocative criteria along with the ability to pay. Thus for any business generating no profit, the liability to tax would be zero but the supplementary rate of tax charged on any profit would be determined by the floor area and other significant environmental features of the enterprise.

Supply lags in the provision of new and refurbished properties reflect physical considerations of construction, combined with non-market considerations such as bureaucratic delays in processing and accepting building applications. Supply can respond to perceived demand, i.e. speculative building, and actual demand, i.e. bespoke building. Time lags are avoided or reduced in the former category although the heterogeneity of business requirements usually involves specific adaptations to a 'multi-purpose' space. More particularly, speculative building itself is an operation undertaken in the expectation of supernormal profits and the nature of the supply lags can dislocate pre- and post-development rental values.

CONCLUSION

The discussion presented here has necessarily been brief and avoided the minutiae of actual and possible policy prescriptions at a national and local level. The approach has been concerned with causal, rather than symptomatic issues. It is implied that there are fundamental causes of possible constraint that have been largely ignored by policy-makers. Furthermore, if these considerations are combined with the categories of entrepreneurial activity earlier, it can be inferred that policy formulation is still a rather naïve process that could be substantially improved. The success of the policies introduced reflects the usefulness of a blunderbuss when the target has not been identified and when the direction of the shot cannot be precisely anticipated.

It is recognized that there are very legitimate difficulties involved with some of the issues identified and, in particular, the dynamic nature of the context. Nevertheless, in terms of economic change and development it is unlikely that policy, or the reallocation of resources it promotes, will be efficient. Obviously political considerations can be very important and override, or temper, an economic rationale. It is relevant to note, however, that the policy options and interventions considered here can be influenced by changes that reflect macro political and economic policy. Macro policies can have a pervasive and major impact on prevailing local conditions: they render the evaluation of specific micro-orientated policies extremely difficult. Macro policies still tend to have short- or medium-term impacts however and need not necessarily disturb secular influences reflecting human capital policies discussed under the subheadings of entrepreneurship and labour.

Policy addressing financial constraints can be more pragmatic although there may be attitudinal elements applying here as well. Enterprise founders who are unnecessarily suspicious of external participation, for example, may set up a business that is dangerously undercapitalized and declare there to be a financial constraint dictating that the operation cannot be financed in any other way. Similarly financiers' attitudes are not perfectly rational and objective. Combined with these considerations are more straightforward anomalies and practices that have become accepted as part of the business environment but which, if negated, could have a major impact on the quality, quantity, and character of successfully realized entrepreneurship.

Significant from a policy-maker's point of view would be the nature of unrealized entrepreneurship and the constraints that prohibit the appearance of entrepreneurial activity. Those policies introduced to date are almost exclusively aimed at new and small businesses that have actually set up. Little attention has been given to those potential entrepreneurs who abandon their ideas before committing themselves completely to the venture. There are clear reasons why empirical data that illuminates this behaviour is not readily available. Nevertheless, the assumption that all entrepreneurial activity is good, while ignoring the notion of diminishing marginal returns and the types of entrepreneurial activity being abandoned before start-up, is not a reliable or efficient route to achieving economic change and development.

TWELVE
THE COLLECTION OF INFORMATION

In this final chapter we recognize the crucial role of information in many of the preceding arguments. This book attempts to combine definitional and theoretical observations on the role and economic contribution of entrepreneurship with a series of specific extensions which enable a more operational and applied view. These objectives of both theoretical discourse and operational relevance necessarily rely upon frequent references to the role of information and its exchange and availability in order to clarify the arguments put forward. At the theoretical level it is the novel use of information which distinguishes part of the entrepreneurial contribution to economic development. At the practical level it is the availability and exchange of information which determines, to a large extent, the efficiency of the production process and the extent to which it reflects changing patterns of costs and demand.

In this operational sense, information refers to individual firms and their awareness of different factor market conditions, those institutions who provide firms with some elements of those factors such as finance, and finally those in local and central government who have responsibility for deciding upon the desirability of policy intervention and, where appropriate, its design.

Since information is clearly crucial at several different levels of the entrepreneurial process, from its inception through its development to its realization, it is necessary to review certain aspects of the information exchange process. While this is clearly in part a matter of policy intervention itself, it is considered here separately, since the operational aspects of policy assumes, to a certain extent, the existence of the minimum requisite information requirements.

The role of information in entrepreneurship is immensely complex and refers to many levels of operation and perception. For clarity, it can be divided into two main categories: information needed by entrepreneurs and information needed by policy strategy designers.

INFORMATION AND ENTREPRENEURS

The role of information from the viewpoint of the entrepreneur encompasses the complex way in which entrepreneurs make decisions. It involves the basis of judgements by them, in terms of both demand and supply. The demand side includes aspects such as market evaluation, marketing requirements, competition, tastes, and many other issues which have been covered in previous chapters. Similarly the supply side requires technological awareness, cost evaluation, and detailed assessments of the implications of different scales of market penetration or expansion.

Information requirements at this level are diverse and refer primarily to the facilitation of communication and awareness between economic agents. The more comprehensive the information set available to firms and individuals, and the greater the ease of access, the more efficiently markets should work.

Like all markets, this process is influenced by both supply and demand aspects. The dramatic increase in the efficiency of communication systems and information technology from the supply side have been matched by ever higher and more sophisticated requirements by users. The speed of change is so rapid that it is almost impossible for firms to make efficient decisions in terms of their strategy for information technology requirements and acquisitions. The greater the sophistication of computer-based systems, the more difficult it is for many smaller firms and individual entrepreneurs to judge the extent to which they might benefit from using them. Considerable investments in time are required, simply to understand the full scope of new systems as they emerge; and knowledge, along with the equipment to which it refers, is swiftly rendered obsolete by new developments.

It is not our purpose here to explore further this fascinating new industrial revolution. The focus here is placed upon information requirements by type of entrepreneur and that which is needed for the purpose of more effective policy design.

INFORMATION REQUIREMENTS BY CATEGORY OF ENTREPRENEUR

Successful entrepreneurial activity at all levels is dependent upon information. The requirements may differ according to the category of event concerned but a general market awareness will usually be common to all. Our purpose here is to suggest the differences in needs which are suggested by the respective economic nature of each category, rather than attempting to encompass all the market information which may be a prerequisite to entrepreneurial ventures in general. Information needs will also vary according to the rate of economic activity just as the incidence of different types of entrepreneurial events reflect changing economic conditions as indicated in much of the preceding analysis. While the constraints confronting the individual will differ from those facing people within a team or established firm, the information needs are similar; it is the emphasis placed upon different aspects of information which would be expected to vary. For example, the individual may not be able to afford the luxury of choosing the precise timing of events to the same extent as a team or corporate department. Consider the differential requirements by category of entrepreneur.

For those concerned with catalytic events the contrast between the needs of a lone individual as opposed to those of a team or corporate group are important. In the relatively rare case of a solo attempt, the information requirements will refer primarily to the multi-market co-ordination as the person concerned attracts the appropriate finance, plant and equipment, labour, and premises. These needs are common to all entrepreneurial endeavours though the requisite pattern will naturally vary according to the nature of the enterprise. For those events which are instigated within a team or corporate context the required information will also refer to general market conditions and those which are particular to the needs of those concerned. In the case of an existing firm, for example, the aforementioned constraints of timing may be paramount. Events may be released strategically according to the balance between launching the event in buoyant conditions to maximize the probability of success and its consequent impact upon profitability, or the needs of the firm to introduce new sources of progress in conditions of depressed markets for existing products and processes. The information on prevailing market opportunities will be crucial to the adoption of an appropriate strategy. It should be noted, however, that the ability of firms to quantify the potential contribution of catalytic events to their cash flow will necessarily be speculative since, by definition, there will be no available data on which to base predictions—the event is unrehearsed.

For the allocating entrepreneur, the information requirements are more predictable since they refer to the Austrian emphasis upon alertness. In this case, the individuals or groups concerned require information on the most recent catalytic events and the existing track record of these inasmuch as it is observable. The prime concern is with the assessment of potential, in terms of the profitability of innovating the catalytic event further. Timing is only a consideration in the sense that the existing proliferation of innovation has exceeded that which is compatible with future profitability.

For the refining entrepreneur the main motive for change is generated through increased competition. Information requirements focus primarily upon the existence of competition and the potential for it to increase. The earlier that firms are aware of changing conditions which have implications for their own trading environment, the sooner they are likely to concentrate on a more effective and efficient use of existing resources. This will, in turn, increase the probability of their survival with acceptable returns on factor inputs employed, in conditions of market recession, as compared to traditional competing firms who are less well informed of the changes which are occurring.

For the special case of the omega entrepreneur who thrives temporarily in conditions of economic recession on an industry-specific basis, the main information requirements concern the prices of second-hand capital, redundant labour, and the prevailing market price of the product concerned. The more alert will appreciate the possibility of short-term viability earlier and thus take a greater proportion of the pure profits from arbitrage as they take advantage of the relatively low set-up and trading costs available. Later entrants will necessarily receive less of these short-term gains as the industry concerned stabilizes at its natural level as dictated by existing cost conditions as a consequence of the reduction in market size which the recession causes.

In short, the information needs and focus of entrepreneurs will refer to general market conditions and market potential but there will be important differences in the nature and detail of requirements according to the category of event with which they are involved. Any attempt to influence information flows to potential entrepreneurs must therefore be preceded by an identification of the kind of event which it is designed to facilitate. The needs of those who may embark on catalytic events are, by definition, unknown. The responsibility lies primarily with those involved, although a general facilitation of information transfer between different academic, technical, and managerial disciplines may be conducive to a higher probability of genuinely new perceptions simply because the information set available is larger. For potential allocating entrepreneurs it is more sensible to increase the availability of information on the latest innovations, but again it is incumbent on those concerned to carry the main burden of responsibility since, by definition, the events with most potential will tend to be esoteric and relatively little known. The same points apply to refining and omega entrepreneurs. It is logical to assume that the role of policy be primarily relegated to the encouragement of access to information flows rather than attempting to focus on any specific cases, since the policy designers' appreciation of requirements will typically occur later than those of successful entrepreneurs.

INFORMATION AND POLICY DESIGN

This second category of information requirement is particularly pertinent, since the rapid increase in policy intervention designed to influence 'entrepreneurship' has been accompanied by an almost complete absence of any systematic attempt to collect information from all levels and types of industry, in terms of their entrepreneurial content and its variability. An apparent contradiction arises when a set of relatively clear policy directions are indicated, but the accompanying research required to provide information for effective design is absent.

It is useful to summarize the nature of the information which is typically collected, and the weaknesses which it reflects.

With increased emphasis on the supply-side approach, and the implications for entrepreneurship both in terms of the political focus and specific policy intervention, there has also been an increase in research into the 'area'. Contrary to the dictates of logic, this research has often followed, rather than preceded, policy intervention. The main tradition of research into entrepreneurship and the entrepreneurial character was established outside the discipline of economics, by sociologists and psychologists, and, to some extent, geographers. As already indicated, the economists' neglect followed naturally from their preoccupation with the neo-classical tradition. Because this analysis is primarily an economic one, the summary of research methods will be almost exclusively restricted to that upon new and small firms, since it is upon these that the main effort has been directed.

The vague association of new or small business management with entrepreneurship has provided economists with a tangible format for research direction. The natural increase in attention upon the fortunes of new and small firms has effectively subsumed the notion of research into entrepreneurship itself.

For economists this is quite convenient, since they can generate relatively robust methodologies which can be applied to research into the condition of small and new firms. The prospect of attempting to provide equally justifiable methods for differentiating between types of entrepreneurial event, entrepreneurial personality, and entrepreneurial culture, while also identifying their relative economic contributions in terms of development, is not straightforward.

Although a great deal of research has been undertaken into the new and small-firm sector in many mixed economies, it is possible to summarize the approaches taken and their weaknesses, in a fairly concise way. The main problem which has characterized virtually all the work in this area is that it tends to occur on a 'one-off', or 'snapshot' basis. Different groups of enquirers have undertaken specific pieces of work, with a particular objective or question in mind. The methodology which they have used is often inconsistent with that used by other groups, and a number of other characteristics tend to make research findings difficult to compare, either between studies or through time. Given the changing nature of the questions which arise, it is understandable that the projects undertaken have often referred to specific and different areas, different industries, different constraints, and have occurred at different times.

Aside from aggregate statistics provided by central government, most research relies upon survey techniques. The two main alternatives are either interview-based or postal-based questionnaires. There is a natural trade-off between the information content and the response rate of these approaches. There is also a trade-off between the depth and consistency of the information gathered and the cost and time involved in gathering it. Interview-based surveys are extremely expensive and time-consuming but provide relatively high response rates with a high degree of consistency in the information obtained. Postal questionnaires are much cheaper and may refer to a much larger set of firms, but the response rate tends to be lower and the consistency of information collected may suffer.

It is not the objective here to consider in detail the various research techniques available for considering conditions in new and small firms. Since it is not accepted that these are synonymous with entrepreneurship as such, it is inappropriate that such a focus be attempted. The main observations which can be made, however, refer to the strengths and shortcomings of each of the two techniques described. With an interview-based survey, it is natural that focus is placed either upon a particular geographical area, a particular industry, or a particular constraint. Although this automatically limits the extent to which the results can be generalized, it does protect the researchers from accusations of inconsistency, bias, and irrelevance, because the response rates tend to be high. Postal questionnaires do enable a much broader coverage. Where they can be undertaken and a satisfactory response rate obtained, the information is often of great use but limited in its detail.

MODERN INFORMATION REQUIREMENTS: A PRELIMINARY EXPLORATION

From this unstructured, episodic, and uncoordinated approach towards research, there needs to be developed a coherent, internally consistent information exchange if intervention by policy designers is to be credible or justifiable. Since this refers to the entrepreneurial experience and content of firms, it would require a survey approach. The main characteristics required are as follows:

1. longitudinal data collection;
2. consistency of information;
3. a high response rate;
4. appropriate, swift, and sophisticated analysis;
5. dissemination according to the information needs of policy designers, institutions, and the firms themselves.

LONGITUDINAL DATA COLLECTION

The longitudinal aspect is crucial for this kind of monitoring system, since it is the identification of changes in the constraints upon different types of entrepreneurship which is so important. Permanent monitoring systems provide an ever-larger database. So long as the consistency of the information collected is retained, the analytical power allowed increases through time as the number of observations grows. This is one of the main characteristics which is lacking in most of the existing research into business conditions.

The growing emergence of a more disaggregated, consistent, if still relatively simple, database would enable the application of more sophisticated time-series analytical techniques. These tend to be far more powerful in their explanatory content, than cross-section analyses. The models which they facilitate can be identified, estimated and tested to very rigorous standards. To date, the application of these techniques has been prohibited by the absence of coherent time-series data. While the nature and types of constraints confronting firms and entrepreneurs may vary through time as conditions change, certain fundamental and underlying relationships may hold, despite quite considerable volatility in many of the other variables involved. It is the identification of these particular relationships which is so important but which relies completely upon the existence of time-series data. Many of the relationships between variables which influence the behaviour of small businesses and entrepreneurial ventures will naturally involve time-lags. As indicated in the chapter on cycles, it would be expected that there be a lag between the incidence of a particular entrepreneurial idea and the attempt at its realization, dependent upon the particular stage in the economic cycle. Other lags of a more mundane form would also be expected to influence investment activity. Changes in interest rates may not appear to affect investment decision-making directly but could, with a time-lag, be identified as influencing it indirectly through the pressures which they place upon liquidity.

DATA CONSIDERATIONS

Given the objective of longitudinal relevance, the major requirement of any information collection and monitoring system of this kind is that of consistency, both in the approach taken to data collection and the content of the data. The changing nature of constraints and problems perceived, both by institutions, firms, and government authorities often make it difficult to adhere to a specific set of information criteria. In this case it would be more sensible to maintain a large proportion of the information collected at each time period, as common to all time periods, but also retain some flexibility to include new areas of enquiry in response to specific concerns or new eventualities. The design of the questionnaire would involve considerable research itself and close, carefully co-ordinated pilot testing. It would require the basic descriptive statistics of size, age, and sector, along with more specific enquiries into financial conditions, investment decisions, innovation, ideas, plans, constraints, and needs. With rigorous testing this can be distilled down to a very carefully structured and clear format, rather than one which is intimidating for the respondent.

RESPONSE RATE

The response rate required must refer to most of those firms approached. This implies the need for some reward or price system. One benefit which has resulted from the historical application of a wide variety of different information collection techniques, however, is the ability to test for those which appear to promote a high response rate naturally, as opposed to those which do not. This again would constitute part of the testing procedures.

ANALYSIS AND DISSEMINATION

A major problem for the kind of monitoring system envisaged is that of the means of data collection. Having designed the appropriate structure of questionnaires this should be undertaken at a regional level. The number of firms required to constitute a representative picture of regional industrial structure would obviously depend on the size of the region concerned, the density of industrial activity within it, and its diversity. These criteria must be determined primarily by the existing local authority and regional authority structures which operate in the country concerned. For example, in the United Kingdom they would logically take the form of local-authority supervision and distribution. Authorities would be provided with details of the methodology to be used in selecting the appropriate sample, and maintaining contact with that sample while updating it as necessary.

Given information collection at the regional level, the results would then be fed into a central point where the appropriate analysis would be undertaken, disaggregated by region, and aggregated for the economy as a whole. The resultant analysis would then be redistributed to the regions themselves.

The information would also be provided to the relevant institutions, either at a central level in the case of centralized institutions, such as in the UK, the major clearing banks, or to local agencies, if that was appropriate. It would also be made available to representative bodies for different industrial sectors, such as trade associations and also chambers of industry and commerce.

This would create a more uniform access to information on the part of those institutions providing firms with finance, advice, consultancy, etc. Resultant competition for business between those institutions would therefore begin at a higher level of information. It would refer to a far more accurate perception of trading conditions and, therefore, enable competition to focus upon the fine tuning of supplies. This would obviate the need for institutions, such as banks, to enter into competition at a lower level of information, and thus avoid unnecessary explorations, often costly, into the marketing of new but unwanted financial products, for example. The market process would therefore be facilitated, since the general level of information available would refer to a much higher degree of accuracy and consistency.

The initial installation of such a system would be costly and require a gradual introduction with constant testing and cross-referencing between regions for flaws and potential improvements in data collection. Once instituted, however, it would be relatively cheap and simple to operate. In economies with a relatively comprehensive access to computing facilities, for example, it might be feasible after a relatively short period of time to have the information inputted directly on line to a central regional computer which itself would simply transfer the data to the central collection point.

The main dangers confronting such a system would refer to the bureaucratization and resistance which might affect the regional collections, and their transmission to the central collection point. It is also sensible to assume that many firms would resist participation in the absence of a reward structure to compensate for the time taken in submitting the information.

The aspect of reward would be most sensibly determined with reference to each particular region. The choice of rewards for firms participating would need to be pilot-tested in each region to discover which particular aspects appealed most to potential participating firms. It would be necessary to offer a set of options to firms in order to persuade them to co-operate. Their needs and requirements would naturally vary but since they would be involved in an information retrieval network, it would be appropriate that the reward refer to information as well. The main objective in determining the options available to firms would be to provide aspects of information or technology to firms which would be costly for them to acquire individually, but which could be provided relatively cheaply by the relevant regional authority, in part, as a result of the information provisions generated from the monitoring process. If the options were designed carefully with particular reference to the requirements of the firms in the area concerned, then it is sensible to assume that a level would be found which produced a co-operative environment. This may be best viewed in terms of a market process whereby the price, i.e. the option chosen by firms, is determined in such a way that co-operation is ensured. There would be clear instances where firms receive disproportionate rewards as compared to the time taken to submit the information. Such consumer surplus is clearly unavoidable in the absence of a very high level of disaggregation with respect to each firms' requirements. Discriminatory option facilities could not be applied in a sensible manner for the numbers of firms required. Coercion would only be required in the sense of a policing process to ensure that those firms who had agreed to co-operate as a result of the incentives provided through the options did provide that information at the time it was required. Such monitoring and checking facilities would operate on similar lines to those which refer to any form of locally implemented tax.

The second danger would refer to the possibility of firms submitting inaccurate information. This would imply an extension of the policing process, with random checks to ensure that sufficient time and effort was expended by firms to ensure accurate inputs. These need not be wide-ranging in coverage, since the fines which would be applied in the case of default in information provision would be set at levels which ensured or guaranteed accurate inputs.

The third danger concerns the analysis of the results themselves, and their interpretation and subsequent dissemination. Clearly the overriding consistency of approach dictated by such a system must be accompanied by a robust and vigorous analytical process which, once instituted, could be operated almost automatically, in terms of deriving frequency distributions creating cross tabulations which would indicate significant deviations from the expected distributions of the data collected, analysis of variance, etc. Again the wide variety of techniques already used in many economies would facilitate the design of a reliable system.

As the system became established, using, wherever possible, existing regional authorities and centres, the firms involved would become more used to submitting the information in a routine manner, and thus learn to do so in an efficient way for their purposes. The dissemination of information, which would at first present considerable challenges to those receiving it, would also become more sophisticated as time proceeded and the number of information releases experienced rose. In particular, it would be expected that the recipients of information would gradually learn how best to use it for their own purposes.

Politicians at a central level would become more aware, both of aggregate constraints and requirements, and of the disaggregated regional differences. Their own centrally determined policies could then be designed to reflect relative regional requirements. This would avoid the problems which often occur in the application of a centrally applied policy, in terms of regional disparities in its uptake and influence. Similarly, institutions would also become more aware of the requirements of firms, and the constraints which were experienced. They would gain access to the relative importance of different constraints and changes in the rankings which were experienced as different policies to alleviate them were implemented. Policy designers at both a central and local level would also have increasing access to the institutions' reactions and their shortcomings. This would enable a more coherent and informed relationship between policy-makers and the institutions which they attempt to influence.

As indicated, the main rewards in terms of information exchange from such a system will naturally increase the longer it is operational. As the time-series for each region, and for the economy as a whole, lengthens, so the level of sophistication and the analytical techniques which could be applied, grow. The extent to which this would occur is determined primarily by the frequency of response required from firms. The greater the frequency, the shorter the period of time which needs to elapse before more sophisticated techniques can be applied. Eventually it would be possible to start determining the direction of causality within specific relationships. This is, at present, largely prohibited by the proliferation of cross-section analysis in researches which are undertaken. For example, an analysis of the relationship between the growth of firms and the financial provisions to them cannot determine the causality between growth and finance from cross-section observations. These will only provide an indication of association rather than the direction of causality. With a longitudinal database such relationships could be interrogated and identified much more clearly, resulting in an identification of the direction of causality and the time-lags involved. Referring again to the case of finance and expansion, it may be discovered that there is an intercausal relationship. Finance might itself determine the extent to which firms can or cannot expand, but in addition expansion itself might determine the level of access to finance by firms. This information would enable more sophisticated strategies and policies, both on the part of local and central authorities and of private sector institutions.

The limiting case for the identification of constraints refers to the causes of closure or firm failure. There has been a considerable amount of research undertaken to determine the causes of failure, but the clear identification of causal influences had been prohibited due to a lack of sufficient longitudinal data. Again the implementation of a permanent and consistent monitoring system would enable a much more rigorous analysis of the causes of failure, and therefore inform policy designers and institutions as to how to prevent unwarranted or illegitimate failure. It would also enable the introduction of preventative advisory services, which could enable firms to avoid relatively simple pitfalls in their financial structuring and operations.

This pro-active approach to information collection would be in stark contrast to the existing methods. Where these are pro-active, they tend to be uncoordinated and inconsistent in their approach. In the majority of cases, however, advisory services and institutions tend to operate at a reactive level. Their perception of constraints in terms of relative significance is therefore primarily determined by the extent to which they are explicit in the responses or demands of firms. This would not be expected to reflect the actual incidence or experience of constraints, but rather the number of firms which have actually perceived and identified the seriousness and significance of those constraints to their own successful operation.

While the actual design of such a system must remain necessarily unspecific, due to the different regional authority structures which obtain in different economies, its incorporation within economies will be vital in the future. In the absence of increasing protectionism, the relative competitiveness of different economies will be determined by the efficiency of information exchange within them. The clarity with which policy designers and institutions can determine strategy and intervention, along with changes in the services which they provide, will be greater in those countries or economies which implement a rigorous, permanent, effective, consistent monitoring system. The natural accompaniment of increasing information technology and communication systems is that of organized and consistent information. For those economies which experience the introduction of such a system there will be a comparative advantage as compared to those which don't. Given the increased returns from such a system through time, due to its longitudinal nature, this comparative advantage would also increase over those countries who have yet to implement a monitoring strategy of their own.

The implications of the points made above, with respect to the increased sophistication of analytical techniques which a growing longitudinal database allow, imply that the impact of increased information will not be a linear process. Indeed, the ability to interrogate an ever-growing disaggregated database of this kind would provide discrete jumps in the sophistication of explanation which it could provide. The resulting higher levels of understanding in terms of the economic conditions which prevail, and the appropriate means of facilitating entrepreneurial activity, would therefore place countries and economies with a longer tradition at a competitive advantage.

A necessary reaction to the impact of improved information technology is, therefore, to generate a greater and higher level of consistent, accurate information exchange. It is no longer sensible for economies to rely upon *ad hoc* information collection on a 'one-off', 'snapshot', cross-section basis. Constraints will not be clearly identified and therefore cannot be successfully addressed.

It should at this point be made clear that the information required will not be significantly different from that already collected in an unco-ordinated fashion by many central and local authorities. It will be collected in a co-ordinated and consistent way and analysed in an increasingly sophisticated manner. There is no reason to suppose that such a system will threaten the individual firm's ability to retain confidentiality over other aspects of its strategy and operation. The need is for a consistent analysis of existing information rather than an extension of disclosure requirements.

Local and central authorities, along with other institutions which supply and interact with businesses, will simply face a clear choice between determining their strategies and policies on the basis of highly imperfect information, or generating an increasingly efficient method for the design of those strategies and policies.

IN CONCLUSION

In Part One 'The Identification of Entrepreneurship', we presented a highly selective set of historical observations which epitomize the nature of the debate about the economic role and contribution of entrepreneurs. Our aim was to highlight the main aspects of apparent confusion and explain how they could be reconciled by focusing upon the different characteristics of events rather than individuals. Entrepreneurship occurs in a variety of forms, each of which is associated with different economic implications. We have chosen to portray the gradations of entrepreneurial contribution according to definable sets of characteristics which they manifest in their impact upon existing allocations of factor inputs. The reconciliation emerges from the interreliance of different entrepreneurial events, the catalytic being the highest order as a prerequisite for the further innovation of these by allocating events. The disturbances which these cause call forth refining events in those firms most affected and lead, in certain circumstances, to a temporary proliferation of omega activity as firms close or shrink, causing a short-term release of factor inputs with low opportunity cost.

In order to pursue the objective of establishing further the role of entrepreneurship in economic change we proceeded, in Part Two, to a consideration of factor market analysis. Here we acknowledged that, while it is inappropriate to *predict* entrepreneurial events of a catalytic form and their subsequent innovation via allocation activity with consequent refining and omega implications, it is sensible to consider the factor markets confronting different categories of entrepreneurial events. In this way it is possible to identify the constraints upon different kinds of entrepreneurial event according to their needs of entrepreneurial experience, finance, and the secondary inputs of capital labour and premises. We also emphasized the importance of entrepreneurial events within existing firms and the poverty of understanding which emerges if analysis is restricted to the case of the individual 'lone' entrepreneur.

Having stressed factor market flexibility as a prerequisite for maximizing realized entrepreneurship it should be noted, however, that flexibility alone is not a sufficient condition for entrepreneurial events. The introduction of the actual events is clearly also a necessary requirement.

The upshot of this analysis required a reinterpretation of the role of entrepreneurship in its contribution to the incidence of cycles in economic activity as originally proposed by Joseph Schumpeter. By introducing earlier the framework of Catastrophe Theory as a useful medium for portraying the catalytic entrepreneurial event, we could extend and add to this position and explain the increasing significance of stochastic events rather than deterministic forces in the creation of entrepreneurial processes at the most fundamental level of economic development.

This reorientation of the macroeconomic implications of entrepreneurial events is necessarily qualified by the important observation that macroeconomic criteria and their policy requirements serve to disturb, fundamentally, the decision-making processes of those engaged in the realization of entrepreneurial events. The natural processes, both stochastic and deterministic, which create entrepreneurial economic development are subject to the shorter term vagaries of economic interventions and their impact upon interest and exchange rates, disposable income, and overall market conditions. The destabilizing effects of such charges will obviously disrupt the development processes inherent in entrepreneurship.

Given our somewhat ambitious objective of analysing the economic impact of entrepreneurship from a theoretical stance through the conditions which arise in practice for the operational implications involved, it was then necessary to focus on policy.

As indicated earlier, there is a considerable problem involved when moving from abstract theoretical analysis to practical considerations. It is very tempting to allow others the dubious luxury of proceeding to an environment of policy design but we believed that it was incumbent upon us at least to make the relevant observations which the preceding analysis implied.

In the last section we therefore considered some of the main policy options and criteria which appeared to follow from our earlier observations.

Those which relate to entrepreneurship itself rather than the factor markets of finance and secondary inputs indicate a need for the integration of commercial information at all levels of the education process, since it is these which will pervade the experience of all who leave it, one way or another. This is not to suggest the simple application of commercial criteria to the education system since this would not achieve a balanced understanding if market selectivity precludes some individuals from knowing how the market works. A basic understanding of the principles involved can be taught at most levels simply to ensure some familiarity with the environment into which the people concerned will be propelled.

Those policy options which refer to finance and secondary inputs are familiar to those already concerned with these areas, but the emphasis described is important since it derives, in our view, from a clearer perception of the economic role and conditions of entrepreneurship as explored earlier.

Despite the central role of entrepreneurship in creating development and facilitating its permeation of any economy via the market process, we still conclude therefore that intervention is sensible. The instigators would include both governments and other institutions. The objective would be far more specific than a general panacea of 'freeing' the market process, if entrepreneurship and its associated development is considered desirable, because there are natural market-driven constraints which, as we have argued, reduce realized entrepreneurial activity. It is also important to avoid the confusion which emerges if new and small firms are assumed to be synonymous with entrepreneurship. Intervention refers to the two extremes of 'political investment'. One is concerned with conditions for the future, the other with those which are immediate but changing.

Consider the two extremes. The first is focused upon the need to facilitate the generation and application of entrepreneurial events. This involves investment in educational and attitudinal policies which encourage freedom of thought, creativity, and imagination. Innovations would be made with a potential return which is entirely speculative in volume, if not, hopefully, in direction. The second is concerned with existing policy and strategy by disparate institutions to cater better for the changing needs of entrepreneurship through the allocation of entrepreneurial events. Here, the requirements vary between economies and through time. Examples are many, such as taxation policy and the treatment of entrepreneurial profit, the determination of skill patterns, the availability and awareness of different financial products, and the level of understanding between financial providers and recipients. These points refer to the level of alertness to change in the short term.

If entrepreneurship is considered desirable then one inescapable conclusion from our analysis is that intervention must refer to these extremes of political investment. One without the other is clearly bound to fail.

If the need for intervention of these two disparate kinds is accepted, there is a further aspect which must be emphasized in our conclusion. Policy intervention in this volatile and essentially unpredictable area of economic change confronts a dynamic rather than static set of conditions. Unless it is facilitating in its approach rather than specific in terms of particular kinds of entrepreneurship, there is a risk that it will frustrate the path of development by encouraging a pattern of exploration and innovation which does not fully accommodate the *natural* potential for change. Policies directed at symptoms rather than causes, designed on the basis of unreliable data, superimposed on confused perceptions, are potentially damaging in terms of their impact upon economic development. Their implementation can only be excused on the basis of misguided optimism due to ignorance or political expediency. As such, it would appear that the objective of encouraging entrepreneurship involves an almost insoluble paradox for policy designers. They are required by political demand to be seen to implement policies the aim of which is to facilitate essentially unpredictable events. Those which occur cannot be attributed in part or whole to the policies which may have enabled their occurrence. Those who introduced the policies cannot claim success and need not admit failure, since the product of their efforts cannot be disentangled from that which would have occurred in their absence. The natural tendency, then, is to implement policies which can be measured in terms of their uptake or adoption by individuals or firms who qualify. The net result for development may be negative or positive but definitely unknown. The return on policy investment is thus relegated to a measure of popularity in terms of respondents rather than their output and, more importantly, the output which is lost due to the distraction of support and attention from those which would otherwise have occurred naturally.

Facilitating policies may also be suboptional, however, if those who design them lack adequate information.

Our final chapter focuses on this central role of information in entrepreneurial development. This is a vast area where we restrict our coverage to the monitoring and information needs which are an obvious prerequisite to any sensible intervention in this most sensitive area of the market process but which has, to date, been almost entirely lacking in analytical rigour and consistency.

By its very nature, entrepreneurial economic development is a dynamic force; it changes in nature and the constraints which are provoked must be understood if they are to be removed via some form of intervention, just as the threats which it may unwittingly create require identification and amelioration where necessary. Some form of internally consistent monitoring process of the forces at work is needed if economies are to anticipate skill shortages, financial product requirements, and other resource implications, in a sophisticated way. The nature of causality in the new economic relationships which are created can only be understood through time series analysis and its identification of changing conditions and their implications. Any intervention which is deemed necessary relies upon such clear information on the movements of economic relationships, to be clearly justifiable at this margin of the marketplace.

Finally, from the arguments and observations presented in the text, we conclude that entrepreneurial economic development is an immensely subtle and often delicate process. To encourage it requires intervention of a facilitating nature to ensure a minimum of unrealized entrepreneurship and only specific intervention to remove, *ex poste*, any of its outcomes which are considered undesirable. Many existing attempts to encourage entrepreneurship in modern market economies reflect an almost complete failure to grasp the complexity and fragility of the relationships involved and which they interrupt and distort with such cavalier clumsiness.

A RESUME OF THE MAJOR TENETS OF
THIS THEORY OF ENTREPRENEURSHIP

The purpose of this resumé is to highlight the main implications which can be distilled from the many observations and arguments presented in the text. The coverage is both condensed and wide-ranging in its consequences for theory, practice, and policy. The main observations are as follows:

1. The apparent divergences in opinion, of the economic nature, role, and contribution of entrepreneurship can be reconciled by appreciating the variety of characteristics and motivations which underlie their realization.
2. Of prime importance is the need to differentiate the character and impact of different types of entrepreneurial event and the individuals who can be involved in their realization.
3. The economic impact of entrepreneurial events is determined by the extent to which they are catalytic, allocating, refining, or omega in their character.
4. While it is impossible to predict the economic effects of purely catalytic events and their subsequent allocation, refining, and omega implications, it is sensible to consider the factor market conditions which confront their perpetrators.
5. The constraints identified from a factor market approach provide insights for those who attempt to design policies which purport to induce or facilitate 'entrepreneurship'.
6. The economic contribution of entrepreneurship, as represented by the impact of entrepreneurial events, will vary according to the rate of change of economic activity in the markets concerned and the economy as a whole. Recession can facilitate propensity for negative restructuring through entrepreneurial activity while periods of recovery and economic buoyancy will be amplified from positive restructuring.
7. The impact of entrepreneurship upon cyclical economic activity is explicable but probably overridden by the impact of macroeconomic policy and it can therefore be short-sighted for any government to purport to

encourage entrepreneurship in the absence of overt reconciliation of interacting factors.

8. For policy designers it is clear that education, training, data collection, and information dissemination are crucial for an effective economic contribution from entrepreneurship via positive market dynamics.

INDEX

Since this is not a reference book and the arguments presented are closely interrelated, the authors provide a summary index only.

Allocating entrepreneur, 40, 43, 50, 59–68, 92
  and capital, 92
  and factor markets, 66–68
  and information, 161
  and policy, 129, 133–136
Austrians and neo-Austrians, 12, 13
  and allocating entrepreneur, 43, 59

Business Expansion Scheme, 145

Cantillon, Richard, 9–11, 17
  and the allocating entrepreneur, 59
Casson, Mark, 16–18
Catalytic entrepreneur, 40, 42, 50, 59–66, 92
  and capital, 92
  and factor markets, 60–66
  and information, 161
  and policy, 129, 133–136
Catastrophe Theory, 27–29, 106, 172
  and Joseph Schumpeter, 15
  and Rene Thom, 27
  and E. Christopher Zeeman, 27

Drucker, P. F., 17, 18, 135

Equity gaps:
  external, 143
  internal, 141, 142
  and policy, 143
Enterprise Allowance Scheme, 134

Finance:
  debt finance, 82–85
  equity finance, 76–79
  external, 77–81
  internal, 77

Industrial restructuring:
  negative, 103
  positive, 103, 104
Information:
  and the entrepreneur, 160
  allocating, 161
  catalytic, 161
  omega, 162
  refining, 161
  and policy, 162–170

Kirzner, Israel, 12, 14, 17

Labour, 94–98
  and policy, 153–155
Land and Premises, 98–102
  and policy, 156–157
Leibenstein, Harvey, 16, 18, 31–39, 41, 48, 114
  and the refining entrepreneur, 43, 59
Loan Guarantee Schemes, 147–149

Marshall, Alfred, 25
Menger, Carl, 12

Neo-classicists, 13, 43, 45

Omega entrepreneur, 40, 44, 50, 59, 92–94
  and capital, 92–94
  and factor markets, 70–71
  and information, 162
  and policy, 136–137
OTC (Over the Counter), 145

Plant and machinery, 88–92
  and policy, 152
Profit
  and Schumpeter, 25

Refining entrepreneur, 40, 43, 50, 59
  and capital, 92
  and factor markets, 69–70
  and information, 161
  and policy, 129, 136–137

Say, Jean Baptiste, 11–16, 33, 37, 48, 114
Schumpeter, Joseph, 14, 18, 22–30, 45, 46, 105–110, 113–115, 172
  and the catalytic event, 42, 59
  and Catastrophe Theory, 15,
  and the clustering process, 110, 111
  and countercyclical influences, 111, 112
Stigler, George, 33

USM (Unlisted Security Markets), 145

Von-Wieser, Friedrich, 12, 23

X-efficiency: 34, 35
  and Leibenstein, 31, 43
  and Stigler, 33